TOP
10
FOR
MEN

TOP
10

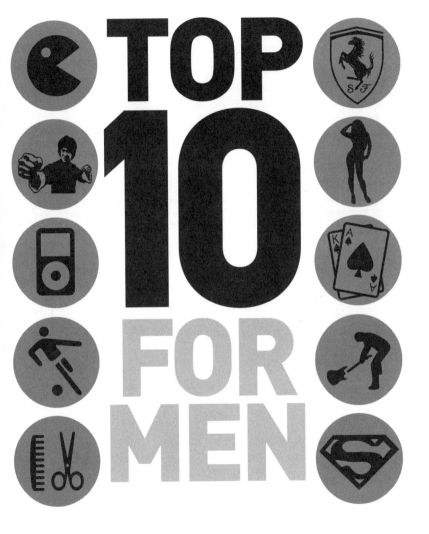

TOP 10 FOR MEN

An Hachette Livre UK Company
www.hachettelivre.co.uk

First published in Great Britain in 2008 by
Hamlyn, a division of Octopus Publishing Group Ltd
2–4 Heron Quays, London E14 4JP
www.octopusbooks.co.uk

ISBN 978-0-600-61817-1

A CIP catalogue record for this book is available from the British Library

Printed and bound in Dubai

10 9 8 7 6 5 4 3 2

Executive Editor Trevor Davies
Managing Editor Clare Churly
Executive Art Editor Darren Southern
Illustrator Peter Liddiard, Sudden Impact Media
Page make-up Dorchester Typesetting Group Ltd
Senior Production Controller Martin Croshaw

CONTENTS

INTRODUCTION

It's different for men

A number of books try to explain the differences – aside from the obvious ones – between the sexes, hence *Why Men Don't Listen* and *Women Can't Read Maps* (no problem, now we all have SatNav) and *Men Are from Mars, Women Are from Venus* (what's that all about?). This book has no such pretensions: it simply accepts the fact that men like lists, so here's a selection of over 250 lists that you – assuming you are a man – may enjoy. They encompass themes ranging from music to sport and from the fastest – and the most stolen – cars to the hottest chillies and the leading baked bean consumers, in which category Britain proudly leads the world. There are many even more offbeat ones: the strangest book titles, the biggest film flops and the highest-earning X-rated films, the most dangerous snakes, sharks and do-it-yourself equipment, the mammals with the highest sperm count (sorry to have to break it to you, but we don't feature), plus lists of preserved bodies and body parts, people who died on the job, as it were, and winners of 'Rear of the Year'.

Nothing like a Dame

OK, plenty of women make lists (I am married to one of them), but they are shopping lists, lists of tasks for themselves or their partners to do around the house and suchlike, not the sort of lists we blokes like. As the compiler of *Top 10 of Everything*, I was once invited to appear on *Woman's Hour* along with Dame Judi Dench, who a researcher had spotted was an inveterate list compiler. The perfect team, she assumed – except my lists tend to be things like '10 tallest buildings' and '10 fastest jets', while Dame Judi's consisted of 'buy tights' and 'go to theatre'. And was it not Bridget Jones whose list of New Year's resolutions ends with 'Stop making lists'? The defence rests...

Men of influence

The are slightly more men on the planet (3,362,269,511 of us, in 2008, compared with 3,317,224,382 women), but, for better or for worse, men are hugely disproportionate in terms of influence and hence prominence in Top 10 lists. As they reveal, the richest people are all men, as are the highest-earning sportsmen – obviously, as they are men, but I gave up trying to compile a Top 10 of richest sportswomen since, after Maria Sharapova, Serena Williams, Michelle Wie and Annika Sorenstam, you are struggling. Every land, air and water speed record has been held by a man. All the most expensive paintings are by men and the Top 10 items of rock memorabilia relate to male stars – it's not quite the same with film memorabilia, but we can guess what sort of men would pay serious money for Judy Garland's ruby slippers from *The Wizard of Oz*. No parliament has more women than men – Rwanda with 48.8 per cent and Sweden with 47.3 per cent come closest, but the UK is way down, at 19.7 per cent. Throwing a discus is the only notable sport in which the woman's record is greater than a man's – but then a woman's discus is half the weight of the man's. We are also the guys who brought you the wars, the mass murders and other stuff like this: hence the lists of air aces (not a girl among them) and worst serial killers (all men) – although, to redress the balance, there's a list of the 10 worst murderesses.

Trivia, not trivial

When I was a lad (I never thought I'd say that, but there comes a point in a chap's life when he's entitled to do so), we used to call our expansive knowledge of the world around us 'general knowledge'. Somehow, in recent years, this has been subverted and is now known as 'trivia', as though it's somehow trivial. Well, it isn't: either you are interested in what's happening, or you aren't, and if you are not you are the less for it. Fortunately, most men – not just nerds – are deeply interested in everything; it's just that we don't want to waste our time discriminating between crucial information, like what are the world's largest countries and even more crucial stuff, such as the most popular types of pizza. Without this data at our fingertips, we couldn't polish off crosswords, hold our own in pub quizzes or sweep the board at *University Challenge* (actually, bad choice – been there, done that, failed miserably).

Size is everything

...at least when it comes to Top 10 lists. When I started compiling *Top 10 of Everything*, back in the mists of time (OK, 1989), I set myself the task of including only quantifiable lists. I figured that if I could measure it (biggest, fastest, oldest, or whatever), and I did my research correctly, the lists could not be challenged – unlike a list of 10 favourites or bests, where my authority to make such a claim might reasonably be questioned. So, aside from an occasional lapse (it's allowed, I wrote it), all the lists here are of things that can be measured and hence ranked – film lists are mostly ordered by global box office earnings, death and destruction lists by fatalities. So, unlike certain other books, instead of just being told what's top of the tree, you get to explore its lower branches. And didn't you always want to know who came second?

Who says so?

I use a diverse range of international organizations, commercial companies and research bodies, specialized publications and a number of experts around the world, who I thank collectively (see pages 287–288 for a full list of credits).

1   R
2   U
3   S
4   S
5   E
6   L
7   L
8   A
9   S
10 H

Please send me any comments (or corrections, if you must) and ideas for lists to the official Top 10 site – www.top10ofeverything.com or to my website www.RussellAsh.com

HIGHEST MOUNTAINS CLIMBED SINCE THE CONQUEST OF EVEREST*

	Mountain	First ascent	Height
1	K2	31 Jul 1954	8,611 m (28,251 ft)
2	Kangchenjunga	25 May 1955	8,586 m (28,169 ft)
3	Lhotse	18 May 1956	8,516 m (27,940 ft)
4	Makalu	15 May 1955	8,462 m (27,762 ft)
5	Cho Oyu	19 Oct 1954	8,201 m (29,906 ft)
6	Dhaulagri	13 May 1960	8,167 m (26,794 ft)
7	Manaslu	9 May 1956	8,156 m (26,759 ft)
8	Nanga Parbat	3 Jul 1953	8,126 m (26,660 ft)
9	Gasherbrum I	5 Jul 1958	8,080 m (26,509 ft)
10	Broad Peak	9 Jun 1957	8,047 m (26,400 ft)

* 8,848 m (29,028 ft); first climbed 29 May 1953

DEEPEST CAVES

	Cave system/location	Depth
1	Krubera (Voronja), Georgia	2,191 m (7,188 ft)
2	Illyuzia-Mezhonnogo-Snezhnaya, Georgia	1,753 m (5,751 ft)
3	Lamprechtsofen Vogelschacht Weg Schacht, Austria	1,632 m (5,354 ft)
4	Gouffre Mirolda, France	1,626 m (5,335 ft)
5	Réseau Jean Bernard, France	1,602 m (5,256 ft)
6	Torca del Cerro del Cuevon/Torca de las Saxifragas, Spain	1,589 m (5,213 ft)
7	Sarma, Georgia	1,543 m (5,062 ft)
8	Shakta Vjacheslav Pantjukhina, Georgia	1,508 m (4,948 ft)
9	Sima de la Conisa/Torca Magali, Spain	1,507 m (4,944 ft)
10	Cehi 2, Slovenia	1,502 m (4,928 ft)

THE 10
WORST EARTHQUAKES

	Location	Date	Estimated number killed
1	Near East/Mediterranean	20 May 1202	1,100,000
2	Shenshi, China	2 Feb 1556	820,000
3	Calcutta, India	11 Oct 1737	300,000
4	Antioch, Syria	20 May 526	250,000
5	Tang-shan, China	28 Jul 1976	242,419
6	Nan-Shan, China	22 May 1927	200,000
7	Yeddo, Japan	30 Dec 1703	190,000
8	Kansu, China	16 Dec 1920	180,000
9	Messina, Italy	28 Dec 1908	160,000
10	Tokyo/Yokohama, Japan	1 Sep 1923	142,807

There are often discrepancies between 'official' death tolls and the estimates given by other authorities: for example, a figure of 750,000 is sometimes quoted for the Tang-shan earthquake of 1976. Several other earthquakes in China and Turkey resulted in the deaths of 100,000 or more. In recent times, the Armenian earthquake of 7 December 1988 and that which struck north-west Iran on 21 June 1990 caused the deaths of more than 55,000 (official estimate: 28,854) and 50,000 respectively. The famous earthquake that destroyed San Francisco on 18 April 1906 killed between 500 and 1,000, mostly in the fires that followed the shock. The earthquake that struck Kobe, Japan (now officially known as the Hyougo-ken Nanbu earthquake), at 5.46 a.m. on 17 January 1995 was exceptionally precisely monitored by the rescue authorities and indicates the severity of an earthquake affecting a densely populated urban area. It left 3,842 dead and 14,679 injured. A further 114,679 people were immediately evacuated, the total rising by 26 January to 232,403. Reaching 7.2 on the Richter scale, the initial shock completely destroyed 54,949 buildings and damaged a further 31,783, while the fires that followed devastated an area of 65.85 hectares (162.72 acres), including 7,377 buildings.

WORST EPIDEMICS

	Epidemic	Location	Date	Estimated number killed
1	Black Death	Europe/ Asia	1347–80s	75,000,000
2	Influenza	Worldwide	1918–20	20–40,000,000
3	AIDS	Worldwide	1981–	>25,000,000
4	Plague of Justinian	Europe/ Asia	541–90	25,000,000
5	Bubonic plague	India	1896–1948	12,000,000
6	Antonine plague (probably smallpox)	Roman Empire	165–80	5,000,000
7	Typhus	Eastern Europe	1918–22	3,000,000
8=	Smallpox	Mexico	1530–45	1,000,000
=	Cholera	Russia	1852–60	1,000,000
10	'Plague of Orosius'	Roman Empire	125	1,000,000

Precise figures for deaths during the disruptions of epidemics are inevitably unreliable, but the Black Death or bubonic plague, probably transmitted by fleas from infected rats, swept across Asia and Europe in the 14th century, destroying entire populations, including more than half the inhabitants of London, some 25 million in Europe and 50 million in Asia.

WORST VOLCANIC ERUPTIONS

Location	Date	Estimated number killed
1 Tambora, Indonesia	5–12 Apr 1815	**92,000**

It has been calculated that between 1600 and 1982 a total of 160,783 people lost their lives as a result of volcanoes in Indonesia, the greatest number for any region in the world. The cataclysmic eruption of Tambora on the island of Sumbawa killed about 10,000 islanders immediately, with a further 82,000 dying subsequently (38,000 on Sumbawa and 44,000 on neighbouring Lombok) from disease and famine because crops were destroyed. An estimated 1.7 million tonnes of ash was hurled into the atmosphere. This blocked out the sunlight and affected the weather over large areas of the globe during the following year. One effect of this was to produce brilliantly coloured sunsets, as depicted strikingly in paintings from the period, especially in the works of J. M. W. Turner. It even influenced literary history when, kept indoors by inclement weather at the Villa Diodati on Lake Geneva, Lord Byron and his companions amused themselves by writing horror stories, one of which was Mary Shelley's classic, *Frankenstein*.

2 Krakatoa, Sumatra/Java	26–27 Aug 1883	**36,380**

After a series of eruptions over the course of several days, the uninhabited island of Krakatoa exploded with what may have been the biggest bang ever heard by humans, audible up to 4,800 km (3,000 miles) away. Some sources put the fatalities as high as 200,000, most of them killed by subsequent tsunamis that reached 30 m (100 ft) high. The events were portrayed in the 1969 film *Krakatoa, East of Java* – though purists should note that Krakatoa is actually west of Java.

3 Mont Pelée, Martinique	8 May 1902	**27,000**

After lying dormant for centuries, Mont Pelée began to erupt in April 1902. Assured that there was no danger, the residents of the main city, St Pierre, stayed in their homes and were there when, at 7.30 a.m. on 8 May, the volcano burst apart and showered the port with molten lava, ash and gas, destroying virtually all life and property. Among the survivors was Louis-Auguste Sylbaris, a prisoner in the St Pierre jail, who later joined Barnum and Bailey's circus as 'The Amazing Survivor of Mont Pelée'.

4   **Nevado del Ruiz, Colombia**   13 Nov 1985   **22,940**

The Andean volcano gave warning signs of erupting, but by the time it was decided to evacuate the local inhabitants, it was too late. The hot steam, rocks and ash ejected from Nevado del Ruiz melted its icecap, resulting in a mudslide that completely engulfed the town of Armero.

5   **Mount Etna, Sicily**   11 Mar 1669   **up to 20,000**

Europe's largest volcano (3,280 m/10,760 ft) has erupted frequently, but the worst instance occurred in 1669, when the lava flow engulfed the town of Catania, according to some accounts killing as many as 20,000.

6   **Mount Etna, Sicily**   1169   **over 15,000**

Large numbers died in Catania Cathedral, where they believed they would be safe, and more were killed when a tsunami caused by the eruption hit the port of Messina.

7   **Unzen, Japan**   1 Apr 1792   **14,300**

During a period of intense volcanic activity in the area, the island of Unzen (or Unsen) completely disappeared, killing all its inhabitants.

8   **Laki, Iceland**   Jan–Jun 1783   **9,350**

Iceland is one of the most volcanically active places on Earth, but being sparsely populated eruptions seldom result in major loss of life. The worst exception occurred at the Laki volcanic ridge, culminating on 11 June with the largest ever recorded lava flow. It engulfed many villages in a river of lava up to 80 km (50 miles) long and 30 m (100 ft) deep, releasing poisonous gases that killed those who managed to escape.

9   **Kelut, Indonesia**   19 May 1919   **5,110**

Dormant since 1901, Kelut erupted without warning, ejecting a crater lake that killed inhabitants by drowning or in resultant mudslides. The volcano remains active, erupting as recently as 2007.

10   **Galunggung, Indonesia**   8 Oct 1882   **4,011**

Galunggung erupted suddenly, spewing boiling mud, burning sulphur, ash and rocks before finally exploding and destroying a total of 114 villages. A further eruption in 1982 killed 68 people.

THE 10
WORST FLOODS

	Location	Date	Estimated number killed
1	Huang He River, China	Aug 1931	**3,700,000**
2	Huang He River, China	Spring 1887	**1,500,000**
3	Holland	1 Nov 1530	**400,000**
4	Kaifong, China	1642	**300,000**
5	Henan, China	Sep–Nov 1939	**>200,000**
6	Bengal, India	1876	**200,000**
7	Yangtze River, China	Aug–Sep 1931	**140,000**
8	Holland	1646	**110,000**
9	North Vietnam	30 Aug 1971	**>100,000**
10=	Friesland, Holland	1228	**100,000**
=	Dordrecht, Holland	16 Apr 1421	**100,000**
=	Yangtze River, China	Sep 1911	**100,000**
=	Canton, China	12 Jun 1915	**100,000**

Records of floods caused by China's Huang He (or Yellow) River date back to 2297 BC. Since then, it has flooded at least 1,500 times, resulting in millions of deaths and giving it the nickname 'China's Sorrow'. According to some accounts, the flood of 1887 may have resulted in as many as 6 million deaths, as over 2,000 towns and villages were inundated. In modern times, an extensive programme of damming and dyke-building has reduced the danger. Nevertheless, in the 1990s almost 70 per cent of the 1,026.7 million people worldwide affected by floods were Chinese.

FIRST EXPEDITIONS TO REACH THE NORTH POLE OVERLAND*

	Name†/country	Date
1	Ralph S. Plaisted, USA	19 Apr 1968
2	Wally W. Herbert, UK	5 Apr 1969
3	Naomi Uemura, Japan	1 May 1978
4	Dmitri Shparo, USSR	31 May 1979
5	Sir Ranulph Fiennes/ Charles Burton, UK	11 Apr 1982
6	Will Steger/Paul Schurke, USA	1 May 1986
7	Jean-Louis Etienne, France	11 May 1986
8	Fukashi Kazami, Japan	20 Apr 1987
9	Helen Thayer, USA‡	20 Apr 1988
10	Robert Swan, UK	14 May 1989

* Confirmed only
† Expedition leader or co-leader
‡ New Zealand-born

These expeditions – which discount any that are disputed, such as those of rival American explorers Frederick Cook and Robert Peary in 1909 – used a variety of methods to reach the Pole. Plaisted's used snowmobiles, Herbert's sledges, Shparo's was on skis. Sir Ranulph Fiennes's expedition, with snowmobiles, was the first to reach both the South (17 Dec 1980) and North Poles. Etienne's was the first solo, on skis, and that of Helen Thayer, aged 50, the first solo female conquest of the Pole. Kazami undertook his journey on a 250-cc motorcycle and Swan was first to reach both Poles on foot.

DEADLIEST SNAKES

	Snake/scientific name	Estimated lethal dose for humans (mg)	Potential humans killed per bite	Average venom per bite (mg)
1	Coastal taipan (*Oxyuranus scutellatus*)	1	120	**120**
2	Common krait (*Bungarus caeruleus*)	0.5	42	**84**
3	Philippine cobra (*Naja naja philippinensis*)	2	120	**60**
4=	King cobra (*Ophiophagus hannah*)	20	1,000	**50**
=	Russell's viper (*Daboia russelli*)	3	150	**50**
6	Black mamba (*Dendroaspis polyepis*)	3	135	**45**
7	Yellow-jawed tommygoff (*Bothrops asper*)	25	1,000	**40**
8=	Multibanded krait (*Bungarus multicinctus*)	0.8	28	**35**
=	Tiger snake (*Notechis scutatus*)	1	35	**35**
10	Jararacussu (*Bothrops jararacussu*)	25	800	**32**

Source: Russell E. Gough

DEADLY CREATURES

1   **Candiru**
Found in South American rivers, they can enter a man's body via his penis and, unless surgically removed, cause painful death.

2   **Electric eel**
Freshwater electric eels can discharge up to 650 volts, enough to kill a human.

3   **Mosquito**
Mosquito-borne malaria has killed more people than any other disease.

4   **Piranha**
Living in the rivers of South America, these small but incredibly ferocious fish can strip an animal to the bone in minutes.

5   **Golden poison frog**
Used to tip arrows, the poison from this native of Colombia is sufficient to kill 10 to 20 adults.

6   **Japanese puffer**
An expensive delicacy in Japan, if they are incorrectly prepared the powerful nerve poison they contain has no known antidote.

7   **Scorpion**
Scorpions are capable of inflicting painful stings, but seldom cause death in healthy adults.

8   **Sea wasp**
Also known as box jellyfish, the sea wasp has tentacles up to 9 m (30 ft) long. Its venom can cause death within three minutes.

9   **Stingray**
Although they rarely kill, Australian naturalist Steve Irwin died when one pierced his heart.

10 **Tiger**
In India, a tigress known as the 'Champawat man-eater', killed a record 436 people before she was shot in 1907 by British big-game hunter Jim Corbett.

MOST COMMON ANIMAL PHOBIAS

	Animal	Medical term
1	Spiders	Arachnephobia or arachnophobia
2	Snakes	Ophidiophobia, ophiophobia, ophiciophobia, herpetophobia or snakephobia
3	Wasps	Spheksophobia
4	Birds (especially pigeons)	Ornithophobia
5	Mice	Musophobia or muriphobia
6	Fish	Ichthyophobia
7	Bees	Apiphobia or apiophobia
8	Dogs	Cynophobia or kynophobia
9	Caterpillars and other insects	Entomophobia
10	Cats	Ailurophobia, elurophobia, felinophobia, galeophobia or gatophobia

A phobia is a morbid fear that is out of all proportion to the object of the fear. Phobias directed at creatures that may bite, sting or carry disease, such as rabid dogs or rats during the Plague, are understandable. Such fears are so widespread that they have been readily exploited in films, including *Snakes on a Plane* (2006), *Arachnophobia* (1990), *The Swarm* (1978) and *The Birds* (1963).

TYPES OF SHARK THAT HAVE KILLED THE MOST HUMANS

	Shark	Unprovoked attacks*	Fatalities†
1	Great white	237	64
2	Tiger	86	28
3	Bull	75	23
4	Requiem	30	8
5	Blue	12	4
6=	Sand tiger	30	2
=	Shortfin mako	8	2
8=	Blacktip	28	1
=	Oceanic whitetip	5	1
=	Dusky	3	1
=	Galapagos	1	1

* 1580–2007
† Where fatalities are equal, entries are ranked by total attacks
Source: International Shark Attack File, Florida Museum of Natural History

Out of 41 species of shark, these are the only ones on record as having actually killed humans. A total of 631 attacks resulted in 135 fatalities.

HEAVIEST SALTWATER FISH CAUGHT

Fish/scientific name	Angler/location/date	Weight
1 Great white shark (*Carcharodon carcharias*)	Alfred Dean, Ceduna, South Australia, 21 Apr 1959	1,208.38 kg (2,664 lb)
2 Tiger shark (*Galeocerdo cuvier*)	Kevin James Clapson, Ulladulla, Australia, 28 Mar 2004	809.98 kg (1,785 lb 11 oz)
3 Greenland shark (*Somniosus Microcephalus*)	Terje Nordtvedt, Trondheimsfjord, Norway, 18 Oct 1987	774.99 kg (1,708 lb 9 oz)
4 Black marlin (*Istiompax marlina*)	Alfred C. Glassell Jr, Cabo Blanco, Peru, 4 Aug 1953	707.61 kg (1,560 lb)
5 Bluefin tuna (*Thunnus thynnus*)	Ken Fraser, Aulds Cove, Nova Scotia, Canada, 26 Oct 1979	678.58 kg (1,496 lb)
6 Atlantic blue marlin (*Makaira nigricans*)	Paulo Amorim, Vitoria, Brazil, 29 Feb 1992	636.99 kg (1,402 lb 2 oz)

7	Pacific blue marlin (*Makaira nigricans*)	Jay W. de Beaubien, Kaaiwi Point, Kona, Hawaii, USA, 31 May 1982	**624.14 kg (1,376 lb)**
8	Sixgilled shark (*Hexanchus griseus*)	Clemens Rump, Ascension Island, 21 Nov 2002	**588.76 kg (1,298 lb)**
9	Great hammerhead shark (*Sphyrna mokarran*)	Bucky Dennis, Boca Grande, Florida, USA, 23 May 2006	**580.60 kg (1,280 lb)**
10	Shortfin mako shark (*Isurus oxyrinchus*)	Luke Sweeney, Chatham, Massachusetts, USA, 21 July 2001	**553.84 kg (1,221 lb)**

HEAVIEST FRESHWATER FISH CAUGHT

	Fish/scientific name	Angler/location/date	Weight
1	White sturgeon (*Acipenser transmontanus*)	Joey Pallotta III, Benicia, California, USA, 9 Jul 1983	**212.28 kg** **(468 lb)**
2	Alligator gar (*Atractosteus spatula*)	Bill Valverde, Rio Grande, Texas, USA, 2 Dec 1951	**126.55 kg** **(279 lb)**
3	Nile perch (*Lates niloticus*)	William Toth, Lake Nasser, Egypt, 20 Dec 2000	**104.32 kg** **(230 lb)**
4	Beluga sturgeon (*Huso huso*)	Ms Merete Lehne, Guryev, Kazakhstan, 3 May 1993	**102 kg** **(224 lb 13 oz)**
5	Mekong giant catfish (*Pangasianodon gigas*)	Tim Webb, Bung Sam San Lake, Thailand, 28 Feb 2007	**79.56 kg** **(175 lb 6 oz)**
6	Blue catfish (*Ictalurus furcatus*)	Timothy E. Pruitt, Mississippi River, Alton, Illinois, USA, 21 May 2005	**56.25 kg** **(124 lb)**

7	Flathead catfish (*Pylodictis olivaris*)	Ken Paulie, Elk City Reservoir, Kansas, USA, 14 May 1998	**55.79 kg** **(123 lb)**
8	Redtailed catfish (*Phractocephalus hemioliopteru*)	Jorge Masullo de Aguiar, Rio Negro, Brazil, 6 Oct 2007	**51.51kg** **(113 lb 9 oz)**
9	Chinook salmon (*Oncorhynchus tshawytscha*)	Les Anderson, Kenai River, Alaska, USA, 17 May 1985	**44.20 kg** **(97 lb 4 oz)**
10	Giant tigerfish (*Hydrocynus goliath*)	Raymond Houtmans, Zaïre River, Kinshasa, Zaïre, 9 Jul 1988	**44 kg** **(97 lb)**

On 1 May 2005 a team of five anglers on the Mekong River, Thailand, caught a Mekong giant catfish weighing 293 kg (646 lb), making it the largest freshwater fish ever, but it has not been ratified by the International Game Fish Association, so the entry at No. 5, at a little over a third the size, is considered the official record-holder. The sturgeon caught by 21-year-old Joey Pallotta was 2.74 m (9 ft) long; as it is now illegal to keep a fish over 1.83 m (6 ft) in length, the record will probably never be broken. The largest freshwater fish caught in the UK was a 29.03-kg (64-lb), 1.37-m (54-in) salmon hooked by 32-year-old Georgina W. Ballantine on the River Tay, Scotland on 7 October 1922. It was donated to the Perth Royal Infirmary to feed the patients.

Source: International Game Fish Association

PEDIGREE DOG BREEDS IN THE UK

	Breed	Number registered by the Kennel Club
1	Labrador retriever	45,079
2	Cocker spaniel	20,883
3	English springer spaniel	14,702
4	Staffordshire bull terrier	12,167
5	German shepherd (Alsatian)	12,116
6	Cavalier King Charles spaniel	11,422
7	Golden retriever	9,557
8	Border terrier	8,814
9	West Highland white terrier	8,309
10	Boxer	8,191

Source: The Kennel Club, 2007

DOGS' NAMES IN THE UK

1   Molly
2   Jack
3   Holly
4   Max
5   Buster
6   Lucy
7   Jake
8   Barney
9   Charlie
10 Sam

Source: RSPCA 2006 survey

TOP 10
DEADLIEST SPIDERS

	Spider/scientific name	Range
1	Banana spider (*Phonenutria nigriventer*)	Central and South America
2	Sydney funnel web (*Atrax robustus*)	Australia
3	Wolf spider (*Lycosa raptoria/erythrognatha*)	Central and South America
4	Black widow (*Latrodectus* species)	Widespread
5	Violin spider/Recluse spider (*Loxesceles reclusa*)	Widespread
6	Sac spider (*Cheiracanthium punctorium*)	Central Europe
7	Tarantula (*Eurypelma rubropilosum*)	Neotropics
8	Tarantula (*Acanthoscurria atrox*)	Neotropics
9	Tarantula (*Lasiodora klugi*)	Neotropics
10	Tarantula (*Pamphobeteus* species)	Neotropics

This list ranks spiders according to their 'lethal potential' – their venom yield divided by their venom potency. The banana spider, for example, yields 6 mg of venom, with 1 mg the estimated lethal dose in man. However, few spiders are capable of killing humans – there were just 14 recorded deaths caused by black widows in the USA in the whole of the 19th century – since their venom yield is relatively low compared with that of the most dangerous snakes. The tarantula, for example, produces 1.5 mg of venom, but the lethal dose for an adult human is 12 mg. Anecdotal evidence suggests that the Thailand and Sumatran black birdeaters may be equally dangerous, but there is insufficient data available.

FASTEST MAMMALS

	Mammal/scientific name	Maximum recorded speed*
1	Cheetah (*Acinonyx jubatus*)	114 km/h (71 mph)
2	Pronghorn antelope (*Antilocapra americana*)	95 km/h (57 mph)
3=	Blue wildebeest (brindled gnu) (*Connochaetes taurinus*)	80 km/h (50 mph)
=	Lion (*Panthera leo*)	80 km/h (50 mph)
=	Springbok (*Antidorcas marsupialis*)	80 km/h (50 mph)
6=	Brown hare (*Lepus capensis*)	77 km/h (48 mph)
=	Red fox (*Vulpes vulpes*)	77 km/h (48 mph)
8=	Grant's gazelle (*Gazella granti*)	76 km/h (47 mph)
=	Thomson's gazelle (*Gazella thomsonii*)	76 km/h (47 mph)
10	Horse (*Equus caballus*)	72 km/h (45 mph)

* Of those species for which data are available

Along with its relatively slow rivals, the cheetah can deliver its astonishing maximum speed over only fairly short distances. For comparison, the human male 100-metre record (held by Asafa Powell, Jamaica, 2007) stands at 9.74 seconds, equivalent to a speed of 37 km/h (23 mph), so all the mammals in the Top 10, and several others, are capable of outrunning a man. If a human ran 100 metres (325 ft) at the cheetah's speed, the record would fall to 3 seconds.

SLOWEST MAMMALS

	Mammal/scientific name	Average speed*
1	Three-toed sloth (*Bradypus variegatus*)	0.1—0.3 km/h (0.06—0.19 mph)
2	Short-tailed (giant mole) shrew (*Blarina brevicauda*)	2.2 km/h (1.4 mph)
3=	Pine vole (*Microtus pinetorum*)	4.2 km/h (2.6 mph)
=	Red-backed vole (*Clethrionomys gapperi*)	4.2 km/h (2.6 mph)
5	Opossum (order *Didelphimorphia*)	4.4 km/h (2.7 mph)
6	Deer mouse (order *Peromyscus*)	4.5 km/h (2.8 mph)
7	Woodland jumping mouse (*Napaeozapus insignis*)	5.3 km/h (3.3 mph)
8	Meadow jumping mouse (*Zapus hudsonius*)	5.5 km/h (3.4 mph)
9	Meadow mouse or meadow vole (*Microtus pennsylvanicus*)	6.6 km/h (4.1 mph)
10	White-footed mouse (*Peromyscus leucopus*)	6.8 km/h (4.2 mph)

* Of those species for which data are available

TOP 10
SLEEPIEST MAMMALS

	Mammal/scientific name	Average hours of sleep per day*
1=	Lion (*Panthera leo*)	20
=	Three-toed sloth (*Bradypus variegatus*)	20
3	Little brown bat (*Myotis lucifugus*)	19.9
4	Big brown bat (*Eptesicus fuscus*)	19.7
5=	Opossum (*Didelphis virginiana*)	19.4
=	Water opossum (Yapok) (*Chironectes minimus*)	19.4
7	Giant armadillo (*Priodontes maximus*)	18.1
8	Koala (*Phascolarctos cinereus*)	18
9	Nine-banded armadillo (*Dasypus novemcinctus*)	17.4
10	Southern owl monkey (*Aotus azarai*)	17

* Of those species for which data are available

The list excludes periods of hibernation, which can last up to several months among creatures such as the ground squirrel, marmot and brown bear. At the other end of the scale comes the frantic shrew, which has to hunt and eat constantly or perish.

HEAVIEST DINOSAURS EVER DISCOVERED

Name	Estimated weight (tonnes)
1 *Bruhathkayosaurus*	**175–220**

Fossil remains of this dinosaur were found in southern India. Estimates suggest it may have been up to 44 m (145 ft) long and weighed as much as a blue whale.

2 *Amphicoelias*	**122**

Its massive size, with a length of some 25 m (82 ft), has been extrapolated from vertebrae fragments discovered in Colorado, USA, in 1877 but since lost.

3= *Argentinosaurus*	**80–100**

In 1988 an Argentinian farmer discovered a 1.8-m (6-ft) long bone. The dinosaur may have been 22–6 m (72–85 ft) in length.

= *Puertasaurus*	**80–100**

Found in Patagonia, it may have measured as much as 35–40 m (115–31 ft).

5 *Argyrosaurus*	**>80**

This South American dinosaur, whose name means 'silver lizard', was perhaps 20–30 m (66–98 ft) long.

6 *Paralititan*	**65–80**

Remains discovered in the Sahara Desert in Egypt suggest that this was a giant plant-eater, possibly up to 24 m (80 ft) in length. Its humerus (upper arm bone) measures 1.69 m (5 ft 7 in), 14 per cent longer than that of any dinosaur previously discovered.

7 *Antarctosaurus*	**69**

This name, which means 'southern lizard', was coined in 1929 by German palaeontologist Friedrich von Huene. The creature's thigh bone alone measures 2.3 m (7 ft 6 in) and a total length of 18 m (60 ft) has been estimated. Some authorities have put its weight as high as 80 tonnes.

8   *Sauroposeidon*   **50—60**

Known only from vertebrae discovered in Oklahoma, USA, in 1994, this may have been the tallest of all dinosaurs at 17 m (55 ft 10 in).

9   *Brachiosaurus*   **48—56**

This name, which means 'arm lizard', was coined in 1903 by US palaeontologist Elmer S. Riggs. Some palaeontologists have suggested the dinosaur, which was 25 m (82 ft) long, weighed as much as 190 tonnes, but this seems improbable (if not impossible, in the light of theories of the maximum possible weight of terrestrial animals).

10 *Supersaurus*   **40—50**

Fragments of *Supersaurus* were unearthed in Colorado, USA, in 1972. It may have measured up to 40 m (130 ft) long. Another specimen, known as 'Jimbo', has been discovered in Wyoming, USA, and is undergoing examination.

Everyone's favourite dinosaur, *Tyrannosaurus rex* ('tyrant lizard'), does not appear in the Top 10 list because although it was one of the fiercest flesh-eating dinosaurs, it was not as large as many of the herbivorous ones. However, measuring a probable 12 m (39 ft) and weighing more than six tonnes, it certainly ranks as one of the largest flesh-eating animals yet discovered. Bones of an earlier dinosaur called *Epanterias* were found in Colorado in 1877 and 1934, but incorrectly identified until recently, when studies suggested that this creature was possibly larger than *Tyrannosaurus*.

To compare these sizes with living animals, note that the largest recorded crocodile measured 6.2 m (20 ft 4 in) and the largest elephant 10.7 m (35 ft) from trunk to tail and weighed about 12 tonnes. The largest living creature ever measured is the blue whale at 33.6 m (110 ft) – smaller than the size claimed for some in this list.

LONGEST SNAKES

	Snake/scientific name	Maximum length
1	Reticulated (royal) python (*Python reticulatus*)	10 m (32 ft)
2	Anaconda (*Eunectes murinus*)	8.5 m (28 ft)
3	Indian python (*Python molurus molurus*)	7.6 m (25 ft)
4	Diamond python (*Morelia spilota spilota*)	6.4 m (21 ft)
5	King cobra (*Opiophagus hannah*)	5.8 m (19 ft)
6	Boa constrictor (*Boa constrictor*)	4.9 m (16 ft)
7	Bushmaster (*Lachesis muta*)	3.7 m (12 ft)
8	Giant brown snake (*Oxyuranus scutellatus*)	3.4 m (11 ft)
9	Diamondback rattlesnake (*Crotalus atrox*)	2.7 m (9 ft)
10	Indigo or gopher snake (*Drymarchon corais*)	2.4 m (8 ft)

Although the South American anaconda is sometimes claimed to be the longest snake, this has never been authenticated: reports of monsters up to 36.5 m (120 ft) have been published, but without material evidence. Former US president and hunting enthusiast Theodore Roosevelt once offered $5,000 to anyone who could produce the skin or vertebrae of an anaconda that was more than 9 m (30 ft) long, but the prize was never claimed and it seems that the reticulated or royal python retains its pre-eminence. The four largest snakes are all constrictors; the king cobra is the longest venomous snake.

FASTEST FLYING INSECTS

	Insect*/scientific name	Maximum recorded speed
1	Hawkmoth (*Sphingidae*)	53.6 km/h (33.3 mph)
2=	Deer botfly (*Cephenemyia pratti*)	48 km/h (30 mph)
=	West Indian butterfly (*Nymphalidae prepona*)	48 km/h (30 mph)
4	Deer bot fly (*Chrysops*)	40 km/h (25 mph)
5	West Indian butterfly (*Hesperiidae sp.*)	39 km/h (24.2 mph)
6	Lesser Emperor dragonfly (*Anax parthenope*)	28.6 km/h (17.8 mph)
7=	Dragonfly (*Aeschna*)	25.2 km/h (15.6 mph)
=	Hornet (*Vespa*)	25.2 km/h (15.6 mph)
9=	Honey bee (*Apis millefera*)	22.4 km/h (13.9 mph)
=	Horsefly (*Tabanus bovinus*)	22.4 km/h (13.9 mph)

* Of those species for which data are available

Few accurate assessments of the flying speeds of insects have been attempted and this Top 10 represents only the results of the handful of scientific studies widely recognized by entomologists. Some experts have also suggested that the male horsefly (*Hybomitra linei wrighti*) is capable of travelling at 145 km/h (90 mph) when in pursuit of a female, while there are exceptional one-off examples, such as the dragonfly allegedly recorded in 1917 by Dr Robert J. Tilyard flying at 98 km/h (61 mph). Many so-called records are clearly flawed, however: for example, Charles Townsend estimated the flying speed of the deer botfly at an unbelievable 1,317 km/h (818 mph). If true, it would have broken the sound barrier!

LARGEST SPIDERS

	Spider	Leg span
1	Huntsman spider (*Heteropoda maxima*)	300 mm (11.8 in)
2	Brazilian salmon pink (*Lasiodora parahybana*)	270 mm (10.6 in)
3	Brazilian ginat tawny red (*Grammostola mollicoma*)	260 mm (10.2 in)
4=	Goliath tarantula or bird-eating spider (*Theraphosa blondi*)	254 mm (10 in)
=	Wolf spider (*Cupiennius sallei*)	254 mm (10 in)
6=	Purple bloom bird-eating spider (*Xenesthis immanis*)	230 mm (9.1 in)
=	*Xenesthis monstrosa*	230 mm (9.1 in)
8	Hercules baboon (*Hysterocrates hercules*)	203 mm (8 in)
9	*Hysterocrates sp.*	178 mm (7 in)
10	*Tegenaria parietina*	140 mm (5.5 in)

It should be noted that although these represent the average leg spans of the world's largest spiders, their body size is often considerably smaller: for example, that of the *Lasiodora*, found in Brazil, is around 9 cm (3.6 in), while that of the *Tegenaria parietina*, the largest spider found in Britain, may measure as little as 18 mm (0.7 in).

MAMMALS WITH THE HIGHEST SPERM COUNT

	Mammal	Sperm per ejaculation
1	Pig	60–80,000,000,000
2	Donkey	14,500,000,000
3	Horse	11,000,000,000
4	Bull	5–10,000,000,000
5	Zebu	5,000,000,000
6	Buffalo	3,400,000,000
7	Ram	3,000,000,000
8	Goat	2–3,000,000,000
9	Dog	2,000,000,000
10	Rhesus monkey	1,000,000,000
	Human	*200–500,000,000*

HIGHEST CALORIE-CONSUMING COUNTRIES

	Country	Average daily calorie consumption per capita
1	USA	3,760
2	Portugal	3,750
3	Austria	3,740
4	Italy	3,730
5	Greece	3,720
6	Luxembourg	3,710
7	Ireland	3,670
8=	Canada	3,630
=	France	3,630
10	Romania	3,620
	UK	*3,460*

Source: Food and Agriculture Organization of the United Nations

The daily calorie requirement of the average man is 2,700 and the average woman 2,500. Inactive people need fewer, while those engaged in heavy labour might need to increase, perhaps even doubling, these figures. Calories that are not consumed as energy turn to fat – which is why calorie-counting is one of the key aspects of most diets. The high calorie intake of certain countries reflects the high proportion of starchy foods, such as potatoes, bread and pasta, in the national diet. In many Western countries, though, the high figures simply reflect over-eating – especially since they are averages that include men, women and children, suggesting that large numbers of people are greatly exceeding them. While weight-watchers of the West guzzle their way through 30 per cent more than they need, most countries in Western Europe consuming more than 3,000 calories per head, the daily calorie consumption in over 10 of the poorest African nations falls below 2,000, with that of Eritrea standing at just 40 per cent of the USA figure.

LOWEST CALORIE-CONSUMING COUNTRIES

	Country	Average daily calorie consumption per capita
1	Eritrea	1,500
2	Democratic Republic of Congo	1,590
3	Burundi	1,660
4	Comoros	1,770
5	Ethiopia	1,850
6	Takikistan	1,900
7	Sierra Leone	1,910
8	Liberia	1,930
9	Zambia	1,950
10=	Central African Republic	1,960
=	Tanzania	1,960

Source: Food and Agriculture Organization of the United Nations

HIGHEST FAT-CONSUMING COUNTRIES

	Country	Average daily fat consumption per capita
1	France	157 g (5.53 oz)
2	Austria	154 g (5.43 oz)
3=	Belgium	149 g (5.25 oz)
=	Italy	149 g (5.25 oz)
=	Spain	149 g (5.25 oz)
=	Switzerland	149 g (5.25 oz)
7	USA	144 g (5.07 oz)
8=	Canada	141 g (4.97 oz)
=	Hungary	141 g (4.97 oz)
10=	Greece	140 g (4.93 oz)
=	Norway	140 g (4.93 oz)
	UK	*127 g (4.47 oz)*

Source: Food and Agriculture Organization of the United Nations

LOWEST FAT-CONSUMING COUNTRIES

	Country	Average daily fat consumption per capita
1	Burundi	11 g (0.38 oz)
2	Rwanda	16 g (0.56 oz)
3	Ethiopia	21 g (0.74 oz)
4=	Bangladesh	25 g (0.88 oz)
=	Democratic Republic of Congo	25 g (0.88 oz)
6=	Laos	28 g (0.98 oz)
=	Madagascar	28 g (0.98 oz)
8	Zambia	29 g (1.02 oz)
9	Eritrea	30 g (1.05 oz)
10	Mozambique	31 g (1.09 oz)

Source: Food and Agricultural Organization of the United Nations

MOST OBESE COUNTRIES

	Country	Percentage of obese adults* Men	Women
1	Nauru	79.3	77.9
2	Tonga	46.6	70.3
3	Samoa	32.9	63
4	Jordan†	32.7	59.8
5	Qatar	34.6	45.3
6	Saudi Arabia	26.4	44
7	Lebanon	36.3	38.3
8	Paraguay	22.9	35.7
9	Albania†	22.8	35.6
10	Malta	22	35
	USA	*31.1*	*33.2*
	Scotland	*22.4*	*26*
	England	*23.1*	*24.3*
	Wales	*18*	*18*

* Ranked by percentage of obese women (those with a BMI greater than 30)
† Urban population only
Source: International Obesity Task Force (IOTF)

HEALTH AND FITNESS

MOST EFFECTIVE
KEEP-FIT ACTIVITIES

1 Swimming

2 Cycling

3 Rowing

4 Gymnastics

5 Judo

6 Dancing

7 Football

8 Jogging

9 Walking (briskly!)

10 Squash

These are the sports and activities recommended by keep-fit experts as the best means of acquiring all-round fitness, building stamina and strength and increasing suppleness.

DIY TOOLS MOST OFTEN INVOLVED IN ACCIDENTS IN UK HOMES

	Tool	Accidents*
1	Knife (non-domestic)	15,208
2	Saw (excluding circular and straight-blade saws)	8,764
3	Straight-blade saw (e.g. hacksaw)	5,766
4	Hammer or mallet	5,605
5	Scalpel or blade (in holder)	5,462
6	Chisel	4,070
7	Angle grinder	4,284
8=	Power drill	2,892
=	Screwdriver	2,892
10	Circular saw	2,606

* National estimates based on actual Home Accident Surveillance System figures for sample population

MOST COMMON ELEMENTS IN THE HUMAN BODY

	Element	Symbol	Average adult* total
1	Oxygen†	O	48,800 g (1,721 oz)
2	Carbon	C	18,400 g (649 oz)
3	Hydrogen†	H	8,000 g (282 oz)
4	Nitrogen	N	2,080 g (73 oz)
5	Calcium	Ca	1,120 g (39.5 oz)
6	Phosphorus	P	880 g (31 oz)
7=	Potassium	K	160 g (5.6 oz)
=	Sulphur	S	160 g (5.6 oz)
9	Sodium	Na	112 g (4 oz)
10	Chlorine	Cl	96 g (3.4 oz)

* 80 kg (175 lb) male
† Mostly combined as water

The Top 10 elements account for more than 99 per cent of the total, the balance comprising minute quantities of metallic elements including iron – enough (4.8 gm/0.17 oz) to make a 15-cm (6-in) nail – as well as zinc, tin and aluminium.

MOST COMMON PHOBIAS

	Object of phobia	Medical term
1	Open spaces	Agoraphobia, cenophobia or kenophobia
2	Driving	No medical term; can be a symptom of agoraphobia
3	Vomiting	Emetophobia or emitophobia
4	Confined spaces	Claustrophobia, cleisiophobia, cleithrophobia or clithrophobia
5	Insects	Entomophobia
6	Illness	Nosemophobia
7	Animals	Zoophobia
8	Flying	Aerophobia or aviatophobia
9	Blushing	Erythrophobia
10	Heights	Acrophobia, altophobia, hypsophobia or hypsiphobia

Source: National Phobics Society

A phobia is a morbid fear that is out of all proportion to the object of the fear. Many people would admit to being uncomfortable about these principal phobias, as well as others, such as snakes (ophiophobia), injections (trypanophobia) or ghosts (phasmophobia), but most do not become obsessive about them, allowing such fears to rule their lives. True phobias often arise from an incident in childhood when a person was afraid of some object and developed an irrational fear that persists into adulthood. Perhaps surprisingly, the Top 10 does not remain static, as 'new' phobias become more common: for example, 'technophobia', the fear of modern technology such as computers, is increasingly reported. Nowadays, as well as the valuable work done by the National Phobics Society in Britain and similar organizations in other countries, some phobias can be cured by taking special desensitization courses: for example, to conquer one's fear of flying. There are many phobias much less common than these. Even if only one person has ever been observed with a specific phobia – some more bizarre than others – psychologists have often given it a name, including:

- beards: pogonophobia
- chins: geniophobia
- eggshells: no medical term
- everything: pantophobia, panophobia, panphobia or pamphobia
- going to bed: clinophobia
- gravity: barophobia
- hair: chaetophobia
- mirrors: eisoptrophobia
- money: chrometophobia
- number 13: terdekaphobia, tridecaphobia, triakaidekaphobia or triskaidekaphobia
- opening one's eyes: optophobia
- satellites plunging to Earth: keraunothnetophobia
- slime: blennophobia or myxophobia
- string: linonophobia
- teeth: odontophobia

MOST COMMON MALE HOSPITAL OPERATIONS IN ENGLAND

	Body part	Operations performed*
1	Urinary system	399,321
2	Bladder	278,770
3	Lower digestive tract	273,069
4	Stomach	224,276
5	Eye	199,649
6	Soft tissue	195,545
7	Colon	192,390
8	Heart	184,242
9	Joint	182,704
10	Skin	168,622
	Top 10 total	*2,298,588*
	Total all male operations	*3,174,726*

* NHS hospitals only
Source: Department of Health, *Hospital Episode Statistics*, 2007

OVER-THE-COUNTER HEALTH-CARE PRODUCTS IN THE UK

	Product	Annual sales
1	Cough, cold and allergy (hay fever) remedies	£570,200,000
2	Analgesics (painkillers)	£499,000,000
3	Vitamins and dietary supplements	£441,900,000
4	Medicated skin care	£395,300,000
5	Digestive remedies	£285,800,000
6	Smoking-cessation aids	£83,900,000
7	Eye care	£58,200,000
8	Wound treatments	£34,500,000
9	Adult mouth care	£33,700,000
10	Calming and sleeping products	£25,400,000
	Total (including products not in Top 10)	*£2,473,700,000*

Source: *Euromonitor*

COSMETIC SURGERY PROCEDURES IN THE UK

	Procedure	Gender	Percentage change since 2006	Number
1	Breast augmentation	Women	+6	6,487
2	Blepharoplasty (eyelid surgery)	Women	+13	5,148
3	Face/neck lift	Women	+36	4,238
4	Liposuction	Women	+15	3,990
5	Breast reduction	Women	+6	3,178
6	Abdominoplasty	Women	+2	2,701
7	Rhinoplasty	Women	+13	2,305
8	Brow lifts	Women	+11	919
9	Rhinoplasty	Men	+36	716
10	Otoplasty (ear correction)	Women	+11	606

Source: British Association of Aesthetic Plastic Surgeons

A total of 32,453 cosmetic procedures were carried out in the UK in 2007 by BAAPS members, compared with 28,921 in 2006, a 12.2 per cent increase. Women had 91 per cent of all cosmetic procedures, a total of 29,572, while men had 2,881, including liposuction (582), blepharoplasty (558), otoplasty (418), face/neck lift (230), breast reduction (224), abdominoplasty (98), brow lifts (45) and breast augmentation (10).

PRESERVED BRITISH BODIES AND BODY PARTS

1 ## Jeremy Bentham's body and head
The philosopher died in 1832, leaving instructions that his body be mummified. It is preserved in a cabinet at University College, London.

2 ## Charles I's vertebra
Charles I was beheaded in 1649. When his tomb in Windsor Castle was opened in 1813, Sir Henry Halford stole the vertebra severed by the executioner's axe.

3 ## Oliver Cromwell's head
In 1661, three years after Cromwell's death, his body was exhumed and his head chopped off. It was finally buried at Sydney Sussex, Cambridge.

4 ## George Cudmore's skin
Murderer Cudmore was executed in 1830 and his skin was used to bind a book.

5 ## King John's teeth
John died in 1216. His remains in Worcester Cathedral were exhumed in 1797, when his teeth were stolen. They are now displayed in Worcester Museum.

6 ## Ben Jonson's heel bone
The dramatist died in 1637 and was buried in Westminster Abbey – unusually, standing upright. His skeleton was dug up in 1849 and his heel bone stolen.

7 ## Sir Walter Raleigh's head
Following his execution in 1618, his widow and then their son Carew kept the embalmed head. It was buried at St Margaret's, Westminster, in 1666.

8 ## King Richard II's jawbone
Richard died in 1400 and was buried at Westminster Abbey. In 1776 his jawbone was stolen by a schoolboy – whose descendants returned it in 1906.

9 ## The Duke of Suffolk's head
His head was cut off in 1554 and later displayed in St Botolph, Aldgate, London.

10 ## The Earl of Uxbridge's leg
Shot off at the Battle of Waterloo in 1815, the burial spot of Henry Paget, Lord Uxbridge's leg became a shrine visited by many tourists.

PROFESSIONS FOR A LONG LIFE

	Profession	SMR*
1	Shop assistants	48
2=	Hairdressing supervisors	49
=	Mechanical and aeronautical engineers	49
=	Local government officers	49
5=	General administration, national government	52
=	Site and other managers, clerks of works	52
7	Teachers in higher education	54
8=	Managers, works foremen	58
=	Professional and related in science, engineering and other technologies	58
10	Laboratory and engineering technicians	59

* Standard Mortality Ratio; figures for men in the UK only
Source: Society of Actuaries

Standard Mortality Ratios are a commonly used method of comparing the risk of death in one group with that in another. If an SMR of 100 is the average, then one of 50 is low.

THE 10
WORST PROFESSIONS FOR A LONG LIFE

	Profession	SMR*
1	Deck, engine-room hands, bargemen, lightermen, boatmen	304
2	Hairdressers and barbers	263
3	General labourers	243
4	Foremen on ships, lighters and other vessels	236
5	Fishermen	234
6	Steel erectors, scaffolders, etc.	180
7	Foremen in product inspection and packaging	160
8	Chemical and petroleum processing plant operators	154
9	Travel stewards and attendants, hospital and hotel porters	150
10	Foremen on production lines	149

* Standard Mortality Ratio; figures for men in the UK only
Source: Society of Actuaries

Perhaps as a result of the small size of the sample, the somewhat bizarre differential arises between hairdressers (in the high-risk group) and hairdressing supervisors (in the low-risk group). As the list indicates, workers on ships, and those involved in the construction and chemical industries, with their exposure to hazardous conditions and materials, are as much as three times as likely to die prematurely.

COUNTRIES WITH HIGHEST MALE LIFE EXPECTANCY

	Country	Life expectancy at birth, 2008 (years)
1	Andorra	80.6
2=	Singapore	79.3
3	Japan	78.7
4	Sweden	78.5
5=	Iceland	78.4
=	San Marino	78.4
7=	Australia	77.9
=	Switzerland	77.9
9	France	77.7
10	Israel	77.6
	UK	*76.4*
	USA	*75.3*

Source: US Census Bureau, International Data Base

THE 10
COUNTRIES WITH LOWEST MALE LIFE EXPECTANCY

	Country	Life expectancy at birth, 2008 (years)
1	Swaziland	31.7
2	Angola	37
3	Zambia	38.5
4	Sierra Leone	38.6
5	Liberia	39.9
6	Zimbabwe	40.9
7	Lesotho	41
8	Mozambique	41.6
9	Djibouti	41.9
10	South Africa	43.3

Source: US Census Bureau, International Data Base

MOST COMMON CAUSES OF DEATH BY INFECTIONS AND PARASITIC DISEASES

	Cause	Approximate deaths, 2002
1	Lower respiratory infections	3,884,000
2	HIV/AIDS	2,777,000
3	Diarrhoeal diseases	1,798,000
4	Tuberculosis	1,566,000
5	Malaria	1,272,000
6	Measles	611,000
7	Whooping cough (pertussis)	294,000
8	Neonatal tetanus	214,000
9	Meningitis	173,000
10	Syphilis	157,000

Source: World Health Organization, *World Health Report 2004*

In 2002, infectious and parasitic diseases accounted for some 10,904,000 of the 57,029,000 deaths worldwide. After declining, certain childhood diseases, including measles and whooping cough, showed an increase.

MOST COMMON CAUSES OF DEATH BY NON-COMMUNICABLE DISORDERS

	Cause	Approximate deaths, 2002
1	Ischaemic heart disease	7,208,000
2	Cancers	7,121,000
3	Cerebrovascular disease	5,509,000
4	Chronic obstructive pulmonary disease	2,748,000
5	Perinatal conditions	2,462,000
6	Road traffic accidents	1,192,000
7	Neuropsychiatric disorders	1,112,000
8	Diabetes mellitus	988,000
9	Hypertensive heart disease	911,000
10	Self-inflicted injury	873,000

Source: World Health Organization, *World Health Report 2004*

MOST COMMON SUICIDE METHODS IN THE UK

	Method	Male	Female	Total
1	Motor vehicle exhaust	1,009	120	**1,129**
2	Hanging	835	147	**982**
3	Poisoning by analgesics, antipyretics and antirheumatics	157	162	**319**
4	Poisoning by tranquillizers and other psychotropic agents	101	116	**217**
5	Various drugs	92	68	**160**
6	Firearms and explosives	149	10	**159**
7	Jumping from high place	101	42	**143**
8	Jumping or lying in front of moving object (trains, etc.)	114	27	**141**
9	Drowning	76	58	**134**
10	Suffocation by plastic bag	38	52	**90**
	Total (including methods not in list)	*2,994*	*956*	*3,950*

FAMOUS PEOPLE WHO DIED WHILE PERFORMING

1   **Tommy Cooper**
British comedian, died on stage at Her Majesty's Theatre, London, on live TV, 15 March 1984.

2   **Les Harvey**
Stone the Crows rock singer electrocuted on stage, Swansea, 3 May 1972.

3   **Steve Irwin**
Australian naturalist, fatally stung by a stingray while being filmed for a documentary, *Ocean's Deadliest*, 4 September 2006.

4   **Sid James**
The English comedy actor, star of *Carry On* films, collapsed while performaning in *The Mating Season* at the Sunderland Empire, 26 April 1976.

5   **Roy Kinnear**
British comedy actor, died in Spain after falling from a horse during the filming of *The Return of the Musketeers*, 20 September 1988.

6   **Brandon Lee**
Son of martial arts actor Bruce Lee, accidentally shot on the set of *The Crow* in Wilmington, North Carolina, USA, 31 March 1993.

7   **Chung Ling-Soo (William Ellsworth Robinson)**
American magician, shot on stage at the Wood Green Empire, London on 23 March 1918 when a trick went disastrously wrong.

8   **Vic Morrow**
American actor, decapitated when a helicopter went out of control on the set of *Twilight Zone: The Movie*, 23 July 1982.

9   **Tyrone Power**
American actor, died during filming in Madrid, Spain, 15 November 1958.

10 **Karl Wallenda**
Veteran German high-wire performer, fell to his death while walking a tightrope between two buildings in San Juan, Puerto Rico, 22 March 1978.

UNUSUAL DEATHS

1 **Aeschylus**

The Greek dramatist died in 456 BC when an eagle dropped a tortoise on his head, fulfilling a prediction that he would be killed by a blow from heaven.

2 **Francis Bacon**

The Elizabethan philosopher caught a chill while experimenting with deep-freezing a chicken by stuffing it with snow and died on 9 April 1626.

3 **Isadora Duncan**

The American dancer was strangled on 14 September 1927 when her scarf caught in the wheel of the Bugatti sports car in which she was a passenger.

4 **Anton Dvořák**

The Czech composer died on 1 May 1904 of a chill he caught while train-spotting.

5 **Harry Houdini (Erich Weiss)**

The Hungarian-born American escapologist claimed he could withstand being punched in the stomach, but he died on 31 July 1926 after just that.

6 **William Huskisson**

The MP was hit by a train as the first railway opened on 15 September 1830.

7 **Jean-Baptiste Lully**

The Italian-French composer died on 22 March 1687 after accidentally stabbing his foot with a stick while beating time.

8 **Thomas May**

This English poet was strangled by the cloth he used to support his double chin on 13 November 1650.

9 **Mark Twain (Samuel Clemens)**

Born when Halley's Comet appeared in 1835, American writer Mark Twain died, as predicted, the day after its next appearance, on 20 April 1910.

10 **William III**

It is popularly believed that the English king's death, on 8 March 1702, resulted from a fall when his horse stumbled over a molehill.

LAST BRITISH MONARCHS TO DIE VIOLENTLY

	Monarch	Cause*/location	Date
1	William III	Riding accident, Kensington–Hampton Court	8 Mar 1702
2	Charles I	Beheaded, Whitehall, London	30 Jan 1649
3	Jane	Beheaded, Tower Green, London	12 Feb 1554
4	Richard III	In battle, Bosworth, Leicestershire	22 Aug 1485
5	Edward V	Murdered, Tower of London	1483†
6	Henry VI	Murdered, Tower of London	21 May 1471
7	Edward II	Murdered, Berkeley Castle, Gloucestershire	21 Sep 1327
8	Richard I	Arrow wound, Château de Chalus-Chabrol, France	6 Apr 1199
9	William II	Arrow wound, New Forest, Hampshire	2 Aug 1100
10	William I	Riding accident, Mantes, France	9 Sep 1087

* Includes illnesses resulting from injuries
† Precise date unknown

SHORTEST-REIGNING POPES

	Pope	In office	Duration (days)
1	Urban VII	15–27 Sep 1590	12
2=	Boniface VI	Apr 896*	16
=	Celestine IV	25 Oct–10 Nov 1241	16
4=	Sisinnius	15 Jan–4 Feb 708	20
=	Theodore II	Dec 897*	20
6=	Damasus II	17 Jul–9 Aug 1048	23
=	Marcellus II	9 Apr–1 May 1555	23
8=	Pius III	22 Sep–18 Oct 1503	26
=	Leo XI	1–27 Apr 1605	26
10	Benedict V	22 May–23 Jun 964	32

* Precise dates unknown

A total of 11 Popes have reigned for less than 33 days. Some authorities give Pope-elect Stephen's three days (23–26 March 752) as the shortest reign, but he died before he was consecrated and is therefore not included in the official list of Popes (in fact, his successor was given his title, Stephen II, and reigned for five years – although some call his predecessor 'Stephen II' and *his* successors are confusingly known as 'Stephen II(III)' and so on). Many of those in this list were already elderly and in poor health when elected: Boniface VI, Sisinnius and Pius III were all said to have suffered from severe gout. In addition, the lives of several were far from tranquil: Boniface VI was deposed and Damasus II possibly poisoned. Pope Johns have been particularly unfortunate: John XXI lasted nine months but was killed in 1277 when a ceiling collapsed on him, while John XII was beaten to death by the husband of a woman with whom he was having an affair. In modern times, John Paul I was pontiff for just 33 days (26 August–28 September 1978), his death prompting allegations of poisoning. He was succeeded by John Paul II, whose reign of 26 years, 5 months and 17 days (16 October 1978–2 April 2005) was the second longest.

COUNTRIES WITH THE HIGHEST DIVORCE RATE

	County	Divorce rate per 1,000
1	Aruba	4.41
2	Russia	4.23
3	Moldova	4.04
4	Ukraine	3.90
5	USA	3.60
6	Lithuania	3.25
7=	Cuba	3.06
=	Czech Republic	3.06
9	Estonia	3.01
10	Belarus	2.97
	UK	*2.80*

Source: United Nations, *Demographic Yearbook 2005*

COUNTRIES WHERE WOMEN MARRY THE YOUNGEST

	Country	Average age at first marriage
1	Democratic Republic of Congo	16.6
2	Niger	17.6
3=	Afghanistan	17.8
=	São Tomé and Principe	17.8
5=	Chad	18.0
=	Mozambique	18.0
7	Bangladesh	18.1
8	Uganda	18.2
9=	Republic of Congo	18.4
=	Mali	18.4

Source: United Nations, *World Marriage Patterns*

COUNTRIES WITH HIGHEST PROPORTION OF TEENAGE HUSBANDS

	Country	Percentage of 15–19-year-old-boys who have married
1	Iraq	14.9
2	Nepal	13.5
3	Republic of Congo	11.8
4	Uganda	11.4
5	Central African Republic	8.1
6	India	9.5
7	Afghanistan	9.2
8	Guinea	8.2
9	Guatemala	7.8
10	Colombia	7.7
	US	*1.3*
	UK	*0.5*

Source: United Nations, *World Marriage Patterns*

COUNTRIES WITH HIGHEST PROPORTION OF TEENAGE BRIDES

	Country	Percentage of 15–19-year-old-girls who have married
1	Democratic Republic of Congo	74.2
2	Republic of Congo	55
3	Afghanistan	53.7
4	Bangladesh	51.3
5	Uganda	49.8
6	Mali	49.7
7	Guinea	49
8	Chad	48.6
9	Mozambique	47.1
10	Senegal	43.8
	US	*3.9*
	UK	*1.7*

Source: United Nations Population Division

OVERSEAS HONEYMOON DESTINATIONS FOR UK COUPLES

1. Thailand
2. Maldives
3. Dubai
4. Malaysia
5. Sri Lanka
6. USA
7. Mauritius
8. Bali
9. Egypt
10. Australia

THE 10
MOST COMMON CAUSES OF MARITAL DISCORD AND BREAKDOWN IN THE UK

1   Lack of communication

2   Continual arguments

3   Infidelity

4   Sexual problems

5   Financial problems

6   Work (usually one partner devoting excessive time to work)

7   Physical or verbal abuse

8   Children (whether to have them; attitudes towards their upbringing)

9   Step-parenting

10 Addiction (to drinking, gambling, spending, etc.)

Source: Relate National Marriage Guidance

PROFESSIONS OF UK COMPUTER DATERS

	Women Profession	Percentage of those registered
1	Teachers/lecturers	7.8
2	Nurses	5.2
3	Women at home	4.8
4	Secretaries	4.5
5	Civil servants	3.9
6	Social workers	3.8
7	Solicitors	3.5
8	Accountants	3.1
9	Doctors	2.8
10	Students	1.3

	Men Profession	Percentage of those registered
1	Engineers	6.1
2	Computer professionals	5.3
3	Teachers/lecturers	4.8
4	Company directors	4.5
5	Accountants	4.3
6	Doctors	4.2
7	Managers	4
8	Civil servants	3.7
9	Architects	2.5
10	Farmers	1.4

MISS WORLD COUNTRIES*

	Country	Wins	1st runner-up	2nd runner-up	Total points
1	UK†	4	6	4	28
2	Venezuela	5	2	3	22
3	USA	2	5	2	18
4=	India	5	0	0	15
=	South Africa	2	2	5	15
6	Australia	2	2	4	14
7	Israel	1	2	6	13
8=	Jamaica	3	0	2	11
=	Sweden	3	1	0	11
10=	Argentina	2	2	0	10
=	France	1	3	1	10
=	Iceland	3	0	1	10

* Based on 3 points for win, 2 for 1st runner-up, 1 for 2nd runner-up
† Excluding Helen Morgan, who won in 1974 but resigned

MOST COMMON FIRST NAMES OF *PLAYBOY* PLAYMATES

	Name	Appearances
1	Karen/Karin	11
2=	Debbie/Debi/Deborah/Debra	10
=	Jennifer/Jenny	10
=	Susan/Susie/Suzie	10
=	Teri/Terre/Terri/Terry	10
=	Vicki/Victoria	10
7=	Carol	7
=	Kimberley/Kimberley	7
=	Nancy	7
10=	Donna	6
=	Heather	6
=	Marilyn	6

A total of 652 *Playboy* Playmates have appeared as the magazine's centrefold, from Marilyn Monroe in December 1954 to Sasckya Porto in December 2007. Several have been featured more than once and some with another Playmate.

LATEST WINNERS OF THE REAR OF THE YEAR AWARD

	Women	Men
2007	Siân Lloyd	Lee Mead
2006	Javine Hylton	Ian Wright
2005	Nell McAndrew	Will Young
2004	Alex Best	Aled Haydn-Jones
2003	Natasha Hamilton	Ronan Keating
2002	Charlotte Church	Scott Wright
2001	Claire Sweeney	John Altman
2000	Jane Danson	Graham Norton
1999	Denise van Outen	Robbie Williams
1998	Carol Smillie	Frank Skinner

Barbara Windsor was the first recipient of the Rear of the Year award in 1976. It was not presented again until 1981, but since then it has been awarded annually. The first male winner was Michael Barrymore in 1986 and the first royal winner Marina Ogilvy in 1989.

TERMS OF ENDEARMENT USED IN THE USA

1 Honey

2 Baby

3 Sweetheart

4 Dear

5 Lover

6 Darling

7 Sugar

8= Angel

= Pumpkin

10= Beautiful

= Precious

A survey of romance conducted by a US champagne company concluded that 26 per cent of American adults favoured 'honey' as their most frequently used term of endearment. Curiously, identical numbers were undecided whether to call their loved one an angel or a pumpkin!

TOP 10
FHM'S 10 SEXIEST WOMEN, 2007

1   Jessica Alba
2   Keeley Hazell
3   Eva Longoria
4   Adriana Lima
5   Scarlett Johansson
6   Hayden Panettiere
7   Cheryl Tweedy
8   Angelina Jolie
9   Emily Scott
10 Elisha Cuthbert

WOMEN SEARCHED FOR BY UK INTERNET USERS*

1. Britney Spears
2. Paris Hilton
3. Angelina Jolie
4. Lindsay Lohan
5. Victoria Beckham
6. Christina Aguilera
7. Jennifer Aniston
8. Madonna
9. Beyoncé Knowles
10. Girls Aloud

* On MSN UK and Live.com 6 August 2006–10 February 2007

FIRST NAMES IN ENGLAND AND WALES, 2007

Girls

1 Grace
2 Ruby
3 Olivia
4 Emily
5 Jessica
6 Sophie
7 Chloe
8 Lily
9 Ellie
10 Amelia

Boys

1 Jack
2 Thomas
3 Oliver
4 Joshua
5 Harry
6 Charlie
7 Daniel
8 William
9 James
10 Alfie

FIRST NAMES IN SCOTLAND, 2007

Girls

1 Sophie
2 Emma
3 Lucy
4 Katie
5 Erin
6 Ellie
7 Amy
8 Emily
9 Chloe
10 Olivia

Boys

1 Jack
2 Lewis
3 Callum
4 Ryan
5 James
6 Cameron
7 Jamie
8 Daniel
9 Matthew
10 Kyle

FIRST NAMES IN NORTHERN IRELAND, 2007

Girls

1 Katie
2 Grace
3 Sophie
4 Lucy
5 Emma
6 Ellie
7 Sarah
8 Erin
9 Hannah
10 Anna

Boys

1 Jack
2 Matthew
3 Ryan
4 James
5 Daniel
6 Adam
7 Joshua
8 Callum
9 Ben
10 Ethan

MOST AND LEAST POPULAR BOYS' NAMES*

Most popular

1 Jack

2 Joshua

3 James

4 Daniel

5 Ethan

6 Matthew

7 Ben

8 Thomas

9 Oliver

10 Cameron

Least popular

1 Jack

2 Wayne

3 Jordan

4 John

5 Kevin

6 Bob

7 Joshua

8 Harry

9 George

10 Ian

* According to iVillage, an online information site for women

This list is based on a poll in which people were invited to nominate the names they liked and those they disliked. Such are the vagaries of vote-based lists that the same name tops both.

COUNTRIES WITH THE HIGHEST REPORTED CRIME RATES

	Country	Reported crimes per 100,000 population
1	Dominica	11,382
2	New Zealand	10,588
3	Finland	10,153
4	Denmark	9,283
5	Chile	8,823
6	UK	8,555
7	Montserrat	8,040
8	USA	8,007
9	Netherlands	7,958
10	South Africa	7,719

Source: United Nations

An appearance in this list does not necessarily confirm these as the most crime-ridden countries, since the rate of reporting relates closely to such factors as confidence in local law-enforcement authorities. However, a rate of approximately 1,000 crimes per 100,000 population may be considered average, so those countries in the Top 10 are well above it.

THE 10
MOST COMMON CRIMES IN ENGLAND AND WALES

	Crime	Number recorded, 2006–7
1	Criminal damage	1,185,100
2	Theft and handling stolen goods (excluding car theft)	1,181,000
3	Violence against the person	1,046,400
4	Car theft (including theft from vehicles)	765,100
5	Burglary (excluding domestic)	329,800
6	Domestic burglary	292,300
7	Fraud and forgery	199,800
8	Drug offences	194,300
9	Robbery	101,400
10	Sexual offences	57,500
	Total (including crimes not in Top 10)	*5,428,300*

Source: Home Office, *Crime in England and Wales 2006/2007*

THE 10

COUNTRIES WITH THE HIGHEST PRISON POPULATIONS

	Country	Prisoners per 100,000 population	Total prisoners
1	USA	750	2,245,189
2	China	119	1,565,771
3	Russia	628	889,598
4	Brazil	219	419,551
5	India	30	332,112
6	Mexico	198	216,290
7	Thailand	249	161,844
8	Ukraine	345	160,046
9	South Africa	335	159,961
10	Iran	212	150,321
	England and Wales	*148*	*80,229*
	Scotland	*142*	*7,261*
	Northern Ireland	*84*	*1,462*
	UK total	*147*	*88,952*

Source: International Centre for Prison Studies

MOST COMMON REASONS FOR HIRING PRIVATE DETECTIVES IN THE UK

1   Tracing debtors
2   Serving writs
3   Locating assets
4   Assessing accident cases
5   Tracing missing persons
6   Insurance claims
7   Matrimonial issues
8   Countering industrial espionage
9   Criminal cases
10 Vetting personnel

THE 10

CRIMINALS LONGEST ON THE FBI'S '10 MOST WANTED' LIST

	Fugitive (FBI no.)	Crime
1	Donald Eugene Webb (375)	Alleged cop killer
2	Victor Manuel Gerena (386)	Armed Robbery
3	Charles Lee Heron (265)	Murder
4	Frederick J. Tenuto (14)	Murder
5	Katherine Ann Power (315)	Bank robbery
6	Arthur Lee Washington Jnr (427)	Attempted murder
7	Glen Stewart Godwin (447)	Murder
8	David Daniel Keegan (78)	Murder, robbery
9	James Eddie Diggs (36)	Alleged murder
10	Eugene Francis Newman (97)	Car theft, burglary

Added to list	Removed from list	Period on list		
		Years	Months	Days
4 May 1981	31 Mar 2007	25	10	27
14 May 1984	*	23	7	18
9 Feb 1968	18 Jun 1986	18	4	9
24 May 1950	9 Mar 1964	13	9	14
17 Oct 1970	15 Jun 1984	13	7	29
18 Oct 1989	27 Dec 2000	11	2	19
7 Dec 1996	*	11	0	25
21 Jun 1954	13 Dec 1963	9	5	22
27 Aug 1952	14 Dec 1961	9	3	17
28 May 1956	11 Jun 1965	9	0	14

* Still at large; periods as at 1 January 2008

The FBI officially launched its celebrated '10 Most Wanted' list on 14 March 1950. Since then almost 500 criminals have figured on it, the most notable in recent years being No. 456, Osama Bin Laden, who has been included since 7 June 1999. Names appear until individuals are captured or die or charges are dropped. On 8 January 1969 bank robber and double cop murderer Billie Austin Bryant appeared on the list for the record shortest time – just two hours – before he was arrested.

EMBASSIES IN THE UK WITH THE MOST UNPAID PARKING FINES

	Country	Fines unpaid	Amount
1	Saudi Arabia	319	£29,620
2	China	272	£25,630
3	Sudan	244	£23,550
4	Egypt	210	£20,065
5	Turkey	194	£18,420
6	France	186	£17,910
7	Russia	167	£15,650
8	Afghanistan	133	£12,840
9	Guinea	117	£11,280
10	Kuwait	100	£9,600
	USA	*60*	*£5,210*

Source: Hansard

In 2006, 69 diplomatic missions and international organizations incurred 4,517 outstanding parking and other minor traffic violation fines of more than £1,000 each, a grand total of £418,810, of which these were the worst offenders.

LAST PEOPLE TO BE BEHEADED IN ENGLAND

	Victim/circumstance	Date
1	Simon Fraser, Lord Lovat, (b.c.1667)	9 Apr 1747

The 80-year-old peer, beheaded for treason at Tower Hill, London, was the last person to be beheaded in Britain.

2	Charles Radclyffe (b.1693)	8 Dec 1746

Charles was the younger brother of James Radclyffe (No. 6, below).

3=	William Boyd, Lord Kilmarnock (b.1704)	18 Aug 1746

A Jacobite rebel, executed on Tower Hill.

=	Arthur Elphinstone, Lord Balmerino (b.1688)	18 Aug 1746

A Jacobite rebel, executed on Tower Hill.

5	William, Viscount Kenmure (birthdate unknown)	24 Feb 1716

A Jacobite rebel, executed on Tower Hill.

6	Sir James Radclyffe, Earl of Derwentwater (b.1689)	24 Feb 1716

A Jacobite rebel, executed on Tower Hill.

7	Alice Lisle (b.c.1614)	2 Sep 1685

Lisle was executed in Winchester for her part in Monmouth's Rebellion.

8	James, Duke of Monmouth (b.1649)	15 Jul 1685

Monmouth's beheading on Tower Hill was bungled by executioner Jack Ketch, who had to complete the job with a knife.

9	William Russell (b.1639)	21 Jul 1683

The son of the 5th Earl of Bedford, Russell was executed in Lincoln's Inn Fields, London, after being implicated in the 'Popish Plot'.

10	William Howard, Viscount Stafford (b.1614)	29 Dec 1680

Executed for treason on Tower Hill.

LAST PUBLIC HANGINGS IN THE UK

	Name	Prison location	Date
1	Michael Barrett	Old Bailey, London	26 May 1868

Executed for the murder of Sarah Ann Hodgkinson, one of 12 victims of a Fenian bombing in Clerkenwell, London.

2	Robert Smith	Dumfries	12 May 1868

Executed for the murder of nine-year-old Thomasina Scott*.

3	Richard Bishop	Maidstone	30 Apr 1868

Executed for the stabbing of Alfred Cartwright.

4	John Mapp	Shrewsbury	9 Apr 1868

Executed for the murder of nine-year-old Catherine Lewis.

5	Frederick Parker	York	4 Apr 1868

Executed for the murder of Daniel Driscoll.

6	Timothy Faherty	New Bailey, Salford, Manchester	4 Apr 1868

Executed for the murder of Mary Hanmer.

7	Miles Weatherill	New Bailey, Salford, Manchester	4 Apr 1868

Executed for the murder of Rev Anthony Plow and his maid Jane Smith.

8	Frances Kidder	Maidstone	2 Apr 1868

Executed for the murder of 12-year-old Louise Kidder-Staple†.

9	William Worsley	Bedford	31 Mar 1868

Executed for the murder of William Bradbury.

10	Frederick Baker	Winchester	24 Dec 1867

Executed for the murder and mutilation of eight-year-old Fanny Adams‡.

* The last public hanging in Scotland, though the crowd was held back from the scaffold
† The last public hanging of a woman
‡ Hence the origin of the phrase 'Sweet Fanny Adams'

Public hanging was abolished in the UK on 29 May 1868, after which all hangings took place behind prison walls.

LAST MEN TO BE HANGED IN THE UK

	Name	Prison location	Date
1=	Peter Anthony Allen	Liverpool	13 Aug 1964
=	John Robson Welby*	Manchester	13 Aug 1964
3=	Russell Pascoe	Bristol	17 Dec 1963
=	Dennis John Whitty	Winchester	17 Dec 1963
5	Henry John Burnett	Aberdeen	15 Aug 1963
6	James Smith	Manchester	28 Nov 1962
7	Oswald Augustus Grey	Birmingham	20 Nov 1962
8	James Hanratty	Bedford	4 Apr 1962
9	Robert Andrew McGladdery	Belfast	20 Dec 1961
10	Hendryk Niemasz	Wandsworth, London	8 Sept 1961

* Or Walby, aka Gwynne Owen Evans

Capital punishment was abolished in the UK on 9 November 1965. Welby and Allen, the last two men to be hanged, were executed on the same day but at different prisons after being found guilty of stabbing John Alan West to death during a robbery. The last woman hanged in the UK was Ruth Ellis, executed on 13 July 1955 for the shooting of David Blakely.

MOST COMMON MOTORING OFFENCES IN ENGLAND AND WALES

	Offence	Number, 2005
1	Obstruction, waiting and parking offences	8,216,900
2	Speed-limit offences	2,118,900
3	Vehicle licence, insurance and record-keeping offences	1,195,700
4	Vehicle test offences	284,600
5	Neglect of traffic signs, directions and pedestrian rights	253,600
6	Careless driving	186,000
7	Vehicle or part in dangerous or defective condition	130,800
8	Driving after consuming alcohol or taking drugs	103,500
9	Lighting and noise offences	36,700
10	Unauthorized taking or theft of a motor vehicle	34,100
	Total (including offences not in Top 10)	*12,989,900*

Source: Ministry of Justice, *Motoring Offences and Breath Test Statistics England and Wales 2005*

MOST STOLEN CARS IN THE UK

1   Vauxhall Belmont
2   Vauxhall Astra Mk2
3   Ford Escort Mk3
4   Austin/Morris Metro
5   Vauxhall Nova
6   Ford Orion
7   Rover Metro
8   Austin/Morris Maestro
9   Austin/Morris Montego
10 Ford Fiesta Mks1, 2 and 3

Source: Home Office, *Car Theft Index 2006*

Of the 5,729 Vauxhall Belmonts on the road, 436, or one in every 13, were stolen in 2005.

FAMOUS PEOPLE JAILED IN THE UK

	Name	Crime	Year
1	Simon Dee, DJ	Debt	1968
2	Mick Jagger, singer	Drugs	1967
3	Lesley Grantham, *EastEnders* actor	Murder	1967–77
4	Stephen Fry, actor	Fraud	1974
5	George Best, footballer	Drunk driving, assault	1984
6	Stacy Keach, US actor	Drug smuggling	1984
7	Lester Piggott, jockey	Tax evasion	1987
8	Jonathan Aitken, politician	Perverting the course of justice	1999
9	Jeffrey Archer, writer	Perjury, perverting the course of justice	2001
10	Andy Kershaw, DJ	Breach of restraining order	2008

COUNTRIES WITH THE HIGHEST MURDER RATES

	Country	Murders per 100,000 population*
1	El Salvador	55.3
2	Jamaica	49.0
3	Guatemala	45.2
4	Honduras	42.9
5	Venezuela	42.0
6	South Africa	39.5
7	Colombia	39.3
8	Brazil	27.0
9	Russia	19.8
10	Ecuador	18.3
	UK	*2.0*

* In latest year for which figures are available

THE 10
WORST GUN MASSACRES*

	Perpetrator	Location	Date	Killed
1	Woo Bum Kong	Sang-Namdo, South Korea	28 Apr 1982	**57**

Off-duty policeman Woo Bum Kong (or Wou Bom-Kon), 27, went on a drunken rampage with rifles and hand grenades, killing 57 and injuring 38 before blowing himself up with a grenade.

2	Martin Bryant	Port Arthur, Tasmania, Australia	28 Apr 1996	**35**

Bryant, a 28-year-old Hobart resident, used a rifle in a horrific spree that began in a restaurant and ended with a siege in a guesthouse, where he held hostages, then set it on fire, before being captured by police.

3	Seung-Hui Cho	Virginia Tech, Blacksburg, Virginia, USA	16 Apr 2007	**32**

South Korean-born Cho used handguns to kill 27 fellow students and five faculty members of Virginia Tech before turning a gun on himself in America's worst school shooting.

4=	Baruch Kappel Goldstein	Hebron, Israel occupied West Bank	25 Feb 1994	**29**

Goldstein, a 42-year-old US immigrant doctor, carried out a gun massacre of Palestinians at prayer at the Tomb of the Patriarchs before being beaten to death by the crowd.

=	Matsuo Toi	Tsuyama, Japan	21 May 1938	**29**

The 21-year-old Toi used a rifle and swords to kill 29 of his neighbours before committing suicide.

| 6 | Campo Elias Delgado | Bogotá, Colombia | 4 Dec 1986 | **28** |

Delgado, a Vietnamese war veteran and electronics engineer, stabbed two and shot a further 26 people before being killed by police.

| 7= | George Jo Hennard | Killeen, Texas, USA | 16 Oct 1991 | **22** |

Hennard drove his pick-up truck through the window of Luby's Cafeteria and, in 11 minutes, killed 22 with semi-automatic pistols before shooting himself.

| = | James Oliver Huberty | San Ysidro, California, USA | 18 Jul 1984 | **22** |

Huberty, aged 41, opened fire in a McDonald's restaurant, killing 21 before being shot dead by a SWAT marksman. A further 19 were wounded, including a victim who died the following day.

| 9= | Thomas Hamilton | Dunblane, Stirling, UK | 13 Mar 1996 | **17** |

Hamilton, 43, shot 16 children and a teacher in Dunblane Primary School before killing himself in the UK's worst-ever shooting incident – as a result of which firearm laws were tightened in the UK.

| = | Robert Steinhäuser | Erfurt, Germany | 26 Apr 2002 | **17** |

Former student Steinhäuser returned to Johann Gutenberg Secondary School and killed 14 teachers, two students and a police officer with a handgun before shooting himself.

* By individuals, excluding terrorist and military actions; totals exclude perpetrator

THE 10
MOST PROLIFIC
MURDERESSES

Murderess	Victims
1 Countess Erszébet Báthory	**up to 650**

In the period up to 1610 in Hungary, Báthory (1560–1614), known as 'Countess Dracula' – the title of a 1970 Hammer horror film about her life and crimes – was alleged to have murdered between 300 and 650 girls (her personal list of 610 victims was described at her trial) in the belief that drinking their blood would prevent her from ageing. She was eventually arrested in 1611. Tried and found guilty, she died on 21 August 1614, walled up in her own castle at Csejthe.

2 Susannah Olah	**up to 100**

At the age of 40, Susi Olah, a 40-year-old nurse and midwife, arrived at Nagzrev, a Hungarian village. Over the next few years she 'predicted' the demise of anything up to 100 people who subsequently met their deaths as a result of arsenic poisoning. Many inhabitants believed the woman who came to be nicknamed the 'Angel-maker' had prophetic powers, but her victims ranged from newborn and handicapped children to elderly people and the husbands of many of the local women – in most cases with the full complicity of their relatives, and in some instances with their help. When the law finally caught up with her in 1929, she committed suicide.

3 Delfina and Maria de Jesús Gonzales	**91**

In 1964 the Gonzales sisters were sentenced to 40 years' imprisonment after the remains of 80 women and 11 men were discovered on their Mexican property.

4 Bella Poulsdatter Sorensen Gunness	**42**

Bella or Belle Gunness (1859–1908?), a Norwegian-born immigrant to the US, is believed to have murdered her husband, Peter Gunness, for his life insurance (she claimed that an axe had fallen from a shelf and onto his head). After this, she lured between 16 and 28 suitors through 'lonely hearts' advertisements, as well as numerous others – perhaps as many as 42 – to her Laporte, Indiana, farm, where she murdered them. On 28 April 1908 her farm was burned down and a headless corpse found there was declared to be Gunness, killed – along with her three children – by her accomplice Ray Lamphere – but it is believed that she faked her own death and disappeared.

5   Gesina Margaretha Gottfried   **at least 30**

Having poisoned her first husband and two children with arsenic in 1815, German murderess Gesina Mittenberg killed both her parents by the same method and then her next husband, whom she married on his deathbed, thereby inheriting his fortune. As her income dwindled, she carried out an extensive series of murders, including those of her brother, a creditor and most of the family of a Bremen wheelwright called Rumf, for whom she worked as a housekeeper. Rumf himself became suspicious and in 1828 Gottfried was arrested. After a trial at which she admitted to more than 30 murders, she was executed.

6   Jane Toppan   **30**

Boston-born Nora Kelley, also known as Jane Toppan (1854–1938) worked as a nurse. After numerous patients in her care had died, bodies were exhumed that revealed traces of morphine and atropine poisoning. It seems probable, according to both evidence and her own confession, that she killed as many as 30 victims. She died on 17 August 1938 in an asylum at the age of 84.

7   Hélène Jegado   **23**

Jegado was a French housemaid who was believed to have committed some 23 murders by arsenic. She was tried at Rennes in 1851, found guilty and guillotined in 1852.

8   Genene Jones   **21**

In 1984 Jones was found guilty of killing a baby, Chelsea McClellan, at the San Antonio, Texas, hospital at which she worked as a nurse, by administering the drug succinylcholine. She was sentenced to 99 years in prison. Jones had been dismissed from the previous hospital at which she had worked after up to 20 babies in her care had died of suspicious but uncertain causes, and some authorities linked her with as many as 42 deaths.

9   Mary Ann Cotton   **20**

Cotton (b. 1832), a former nurse, is generally held to be Britain's worst mass murderess. It seems probable that over a 20-year period she disposed of 14–20 victims, including three husbands, children and stepchildren, by arsenic poisoning. She was hanged at Durham Prison on 24 March 1873.

10   Waltraud Wagner   **15**

Wagner was the ringleader but only one of four nurses found guilty of causing numerous deaths through deliberate drug overdoses and other means at the Lainz hospital, Vienna, in the late 1980s. Between 42 and possibly as many as several hundred patients became the victims of the Wagner 'death squad', for which she was sentenced to life imprisonment on charges that included 15 counts of murder and 17 of attempted murder.

THE 10

MOST PROLIFIC SERIAL KILLERS IN THE UK

Murderer	Victims

1 Dr Harold Shipman (1946–2004)   **215**

In January 2000, Manchester doctor Shipman was found guilty of the murder of 15 women patients. The official inquiry into his crimes put the figure at 215, with 45 possible further cases, but some authorities believe that the total could be as high as 400. Shipman hanged himself in his prison cell on 13 January 2004.

2 Mary Ann Cotton (1832–73)   **20**

Cotton, a former nurse, is generally held to be Britain's worst mass murderer. Over a 20-year period, it seems probable that she disposed of 14–20 victims, including her husband, children and stepchildren, by arsenic poisoning. She was hanged at Durham Prison on 24 March 1873.

3 William Burke (1792–1829) and William Hare (c. 1792–?)   **at least 15**

Two Irishmen living in Edinburgh, Burke and Hare murdered at least 15 people in order to sell their bodies (for between £8 and £14 each) to anatomists in the period before human dissection was legal. Burke was hanged on 28 January 1829, while Hare, having turned king's evidence against him, was released a week later and allegedly died a blind beggar in London in the 1860s.

4 Dennis Nilsen (b. 1945)   **15**

Killer of 15 (possibly 16) men between 1978 and 1983.

5 Dr William Palmer (1824–56)   **14**

Dubbed the 'Rugeley Poisoner' after the Staffordshire town where he lived, Palmer may have killed at least 13, probably 14 and perhaps as many as 16, including his wife, brother and children in order to claim insurance, and various men whom he robbed to pay off his gambling debts. He was hanged at Stafford on 14 June 1856. The true number of his victims remains uncertain.

6 Peter Sutcliffe (b. 1946)   **13**

a.k.a. the 'Yorkshire Ripper', he was convicted in 1981 of the murders of 13 women and attacks on seven others between 1975 and 1980.

Although a grisly concept in the context of such crimes, among 'runners-up' are John Childs, who murdered six individuals, for which he received a life sentence in 1980. John George Haigh, celebrated as the 'Acid Bath Murderer' was also convicted of six murders, but claimed to have killed nine. He was hanged on 10 August 1949. Scottish-born doctor Dr Thomas Neill Cream studied in Canada and worked in the USA, where in 1881 he was convicted of a murder using strychnine and spent ten years in Joliet Prison. After his release, he moved to London where he soon committed four more murders, all using the same poison. Known as the 'Lambeth Poisoner', he was caught and executed on 15 November 1892. It is alleged that at the moment of his death he blurted out the phrase 'I am Jack...', which some have taken as his confession that he was Jack the Ripper. (The flaw in this argument is that the Ripper's crimes were carried out in 1888, when Cream was still firmly behind bars in the USA.) The real Jack the Ripper – whoever he was – is also suspected of having killed five. The Moors Murderers Ian Brady and Myra Hindley were convicted of five murders, but are suspected of others. Hindley died in 2002, while Brady remains an inmate of Ashworth Hospital, Merseyside.

MOST COMMON MURDER WEAPONS AND METHODS IN ENGLAND AND WALES

	Weapon/method	Male	Victims, 2006–7 Female	Total
1	Sharp instrument	185	73	258
2	Hitting and kicking	126	14	140
3	Unknown	51	19	70
4	Shooting	53	6	59
5	Strangulation	23	31	54
6	Other	28	15	43
7	Blunt instrument	33	8	41
8	Burning	13	15	28
9	Poison or drugs	24	1	25
10	Drowning	7	1	8
	*Total**	*547*	*187*	*734*

* Includes Motor vehicle (3 male, 4 female) and Explosion (1 male)
Source: Home Office, *Homicides, Firearm Offences and Intimate Violence 2006/07*, 2008

LARGEST ARMED FORCES

	Country	Estimated active forces			Total
		Army	Navy	Air	
1	China	1,600,000	255,000	250,000	2,105,000
2	USA	593,327	341,588	336,081	1,498,157*
3	India	1,100,000	55,000	125,000	1,288,000†
4	North Korea	950,000	46,000	110,000	1,106,000
5	Russia	360,000	142,000	195,000	1,027,000‡
6	South Korea	560,000	63,000	64,000	687,000
7	Pakistan	550,000	24,000	45,000	619,000
8	Iran	350,000	18,000	52,000	545,000#
9	Turkey	402,000	48,600	60,000	510,600
10	Egypt	340,000	18,500	30,000	468,500§
	UK	*99,707*	*38,900*	*41,920*	*180,527*

* Includes 186,661 Marine Corps and 40,500 Coast Guard
† Includes 8,000 Coast Guard
‡ Includes 80,000 Strategic Deterrent Forces and 250,000 Command and Support
# Includes 125,000 Islamic Revolutionary Guard Corps
§ Includes 80,000 Air Defence Command
Source: The International Institute for Strategic Studies, *The Military Balance 2008*

LARGEST ARMED FORCES OF THE FIRST WORLD WAR

	Country	Personnel*
1	Russia	12,000,000
2	Germany	11,000,000
3	British Empire	8,904,467
4	France	8,410,000
5	Austria-Hungary	7,800,000
6	Italy	5,615,000
7	USA	4,355,000
8	Turkey	2,850,000
9	Bulgaria	1,200,000
10	Japan	800,000

* Total at peak strength

Russia's armed forces were relatively small in relation to the country's population – some 6 per cent, compared with 17 per cent in Germany. Several other European nations had forces that were similarly substantial in relation to their populations: Serbia's army was equivalent to 14 per cent of its population. In total, more than 65 million combatants were involved in fighting some of the costliest battles, in terms of numbers killed, that the world has ever known.

COUNTRIES SUFFERING THE GREATEST MILITARY LOSSES IN THE FIRST WORLD WAR

	Country	Killed
1	Germany	1,773,700
2	Russia	1,700,000
3	France	1,357,800
4	Austria-Hungary	1,200,000
5	British Empire*	908,371
6	Italy	650,000
7	Romania	335,706
8	Turkey	325,000
9	USA	116,516
10	Bulgaria	87,500

* Including Australia, Canada, India, New Zealand, South Africa, etc.

The number of battle fatalities and deaths from other causes among military personnel varied enormously from country to country. Romania's death rate was highest, at 45 per cent of its total mobilized forces, Germany's was 16 per cent, Austria-Hungary's and Russia's 15 per cent, and the British Empire's 10 per cent, with the USA's 2 per cent and Japan's 0.04 per cent among the lowest. Japan's forces totalled only 800,000, of which an estimated 300 were killed, 907 wounded and just three taken prisoner or reported missing. In contrast, Belgium had 267,000 in the field, with 13,716 killed, 44,686 wounded and 34,659 prisoners or missing in action.

YOUNGEST RECIPIENTS OF THE VICTORIA CROSS

	Name/campaign/action date	Years	Age Months	Days
1	Andrew Fitzgibbon, Taku Forts, China, 21 Aug 1860	15	3	8
2	Thomas Flinn, Indian Mutiny, 28 Nov 1857	15	3	18
3	John Travers Cornwall, Battle of Jutland, 31 May 1916	16	4	23
4	Thomas Ricketts, Belgium, 14 Oct 1918	17	5	29
5	Arthur Mayo, Indian Mutiny, 22 Nov 1857	17	6	4
6	George Monger, Indian Mutiny, 18 Nov 1857			
7	Edward St John Daniel, Crimean War, 5 Nov 1854; 18 Jun 1855*	17	9	19
8	William McWheeney, Crimean War, 20 Oct 1854; 5 Dec 1854; 18 Jun 1855*	17†		
9	Basil John Douglas Guy, Boxer Rebellion, 13 Jul 1900	18	2	4
10	Wilfred St Aubyn Malleson, Gallipoli, 25 Apr 1915	18	7	8

* VC awarded for actions on more than one date; age based on first date
† Precise date of birth unknown – said to have been 'aged 17' at the time of his award

BRITISH AND COMMONWEALTH AIR ACES OF THE FIRST WORLD WAR

	Pilot	Nationality	Kills claimed
1	Major William Avery Bishop	Canadian	72
2	Major Edward Corringham 'Mick' Mannock	British	68
3	Major Raymond Collishaw	Canadian	62
4	Major James Thomas Byford McCudden	British	57
5=	Captain Anthony Wetherby Beauchamp-Proctor	South African	54
=	Captain Donald Roderick MacLaren	Canadian	54
=	Major William George Barker	Canadian	54
8	Major Roderic Stanley Dallas	Australian	51
9	Captain George Edward Henry McElroy	Irish	49
10	Captain Robert A. Little	Australian	47

The term 'ace' was first used during the First World War to denote a pilot who had brought down at least five enemy aircraft. Raoul Lufbery of the American Lafayette Flying Squadron was the first to be so-called. The British definition of an 'ace' varied from three to ten aircraft and was never officially approved, remaining an informal concept during both World Wars. The German equivalent was Oberkanone – which means 'top gun'.

GERMAN AIR ACES OF THE FIRST WORLD WAR

	Pilot	Kills claimed
1	Rittmeister Manfred von Richthofen	80
2	Oberleutnant Ernst Udet	62
3	Oberleutnant Erich Loewenhardt	53
4	Leutnant Werner Voss	48
5=	Hauptmann Bruno Loerzer	45
=	Leutnant Fritz Rumey	45
7	Hauptmann Rudolph Berthold	44
8	Leutnant Paul Bäumer	43
9	Leutnant Josef Jacobs	41
10=	Hauptmann Oswald Boelcke	40
=	Leutnant Franz Büchner	40
=	Oberleutnant Lothar Freiherr von Richthofen	40

The claims of top First World War ace Rittmeister Manfred, Baron von Richthofen (whose brother also merits a place in this list) of 80 kills has been disputed, since only 60 of them have been completely confirmed. Richthofen, known as the 'Red Baron' and leader of the so-called 'Flying Circus' (because the aircraft of his squadron were painted in distinctive bright colours), shot down 21 Allied fighters in the single month of April 1917. His own end a year later, on 21 April 1918, has been the subject of controversy ever since, and it remains uncertain whether his Fokker triplane was shot down in aerial combat with British pilot Captain A. Roy Brown (who was credited with the kill), or by shots from Australian machine gunners on the ground. Hermann Goering, Commander-in-Chief of the Luftwaffe in the Second World War, was a fighter pilot in Richthofen's Flying Circus, and was the last commander of the squadron before the Armistice of 11 November 1918. He shot down 22 Allied aircraft and was awarded Germany's highest decoration, the Ordre Pour le Merite, on 2 June 1918. He committed suicide at Nuremberg on 15 October 1946.

LARGEST ARMED FORCES OF THE SECOND WORLD WAR

	Country	Personnel*
1	USSR	12,500,000
2	USA	12,364,000
3	Germany	10,000,000
4	Japan	6,095,000
5	France	5,700,000
6	UK	4,683,000
7	Italy	4,500,000
8	China	3,800,000
9	India	2,150,000
10	Poland	1,000,000

* Total at peak strength

Allowing for deaths and casualties, the total forces mobilized during the course of the war is, of course, greater than the peak strength figures: that of the USSR, for example, has been put as high as 20 million, the USA 16,354,000, Germany 17.9 million, Japan 9.1 million and the UK 5,896,000.

BRITISH AND COMMONWEALTH AIR ACES OF THE SECOND WORLD WAR

	Pilot	Nationality	Kills claimed*
1	Squadron Leader Marmaduke Thomas St John Pattle	South African	40+
2	Group Captain James Edgar 'Johnny' Johnson	British	33.91
3	Wing Commander Brendan 'Paddy' Finucane	Irish	32
4	Flight Lieutenant George Frederick Beurling	Canadian	31.33
5	Wing Commander John Randall Daniel Braham	British	29
6	Group Captain Adolf Gysbert 'Sailor' Malan	South African	28.66
7	Wing Commander Clive Robert Caldwell	Australian	28.5
8	Squadron Leader James Harry 'Ginger' Lacey	British	28
9	Squadron Leader Neville Frederick Duke	British	27.83
10	Wing Commander Colin F. Gray	New Zealander	27.7

*Kills expressed as fractions refer to those that were shared with others

GERMAN AIR ACES OF THE SECOND WORLD WAR

	Pilot	Kills claimed
1	Major Eric Hartmann	352
2	Major Gerhard Barkhorn	301
3	Major Günther Rall	275
4	Oberst Otto Kittel	267
5	Major Walther Nowotny	258
6	Major Wilhelm Batz	237
7	Major Erich Rudorffer	222
8	Oberst Heinz Bär	220
9	Oberst Hermann Graf	212
10	Major Heinrich Ehrler	209

Although these apparently high claims have been dismissed by some military historians as inflated for propaganda purposes, it is worth noting that many of them relate to kills on the Eastern Front, where the Luftwaffe was undoubtedly superior to its Soviet opponents, and some of them relate to 'kills' on the ground. Few have questioned the so-called 'Blond Knight' Eric Hartmann's achievement, however, and his victories over Soviet aircraft so outraged the USSR that after the war he was arrested and sentenced to 25 years in a Russian labour camp. He was released in 1955, returned to serve in the West German air force and died on 20 September 1993. All those in the Top 10 were day-fighter aces; the highest 'score' by a night-fighter pilot was the 121 kills credited to Major Heinz-Wolfgang Schnauffer. A total of 25 pilots achieved more than 150 kills yet failed to make the Top 10.

THE 10
MOST HEAVILY BLITZED CITIES IN THE UK

	City	Major raids	Tonnage of high explosives dropped
1	London	85	23,949
2	Liverpool/Birkenhead	8	1,957
3	Birmingham	8	1,852
4	Glasgow/Clydeside	5	1,329
5	Plymouth/Devonport	8	1,228
6	Bristol/Avonmouth	6	919
7	Coventry	2	818
8	Portsmouth	3	687
9	Southampton	4	647
10	Hull	3	593

The list, which is derived from official German sources, is based on total tonnage of high explosive dropped in major night attacks during the Blitz period, from 7 September 1940 until 16 May 1941. Further urban centres – Manchester, Belfast, Sheffield, Newcastle/Tyneside, Nottingham and Cardiff – were also victims of significant air raids in the same period.

THE 10
CITIES MOST BOMBED BY THE RAF AND USAF, 1939–45

	City	Estimated civilian fatalities
1	Dresden	100,000+
2	Hamburg	55,000
3	Berlin	49,000
4	Cologne	20,000
5	Magdeburg	15,000
6	Kassel	13,000
7	Darmstadt	12,300
8=	Essen	7,500
=	Heilbronn	7,500
10=	Dortmund	6,000
=	Wuppertal	6,000

The high level of casualties in Dresden resulted principally from the saturation bombing and the firestorm that ensued after Allied raids on the lightly defended city. Although their main objective was to destroy the railway marshalling yards, the scale of the raids was massive: 775 British bombers took part in the first night's raid on 13 February 1945, followed the next day by 450 US bombers, with a final attack by 200 US bombers on 15 February, while the city was still blazing, with 28.5 sq km (11 sq miles) already devastated by the firestorm. A total of 39,773 were 'officially identified dead', but many thousands more were incinerated in buildings and never identified.

THE 10

COUNTRIES SUFFERING THE GREATEST MILITARY LOSSES IN THE SECOND WORLD WAR

	Country	Killed
1	USSR	13,600,000*
2	Germany	3,300,000
3	China	1,324,516
4	Japan	1,140,429
5	British Empire† (UK 264,000)	357,116
6	Romania	350,000
7	Poland	320,000
8	Yugoslavia	305,000
9	USA	292,131
10	Italy	279,800
	Total	*21,268,992*

* Total, of which 7.8 million battlefield deaths
† Including Australia, Canada, India, New Zealand, etc.

The numbers killed in the Second World War have been the subject of intense argument ever since. Most authorities now reckon that of the 30 million Soviets who bore arms, there were 13.6 million military deaths. This includes a battlefield deaths total of approximately 7.8 million, plus up to 2.5 million who died later of wounds received in battle and disease and, of the 5.8 million who were taken prisoner, as many as 3.3 million who died in captivity. It should also be borne in mind that these were *military* losses. To these should be added many untold millions of civilian war deaths, while recent estimates have suggested an additional figure of up to 25 million civilian deaths as a result of Stalinist purges, which began just before the outbreak of war.

THE 10
NAZI WAR CRIMINALS HANGED AT NUREMBERG

1   Joachim von Ribbentrop, 53, former Ambassador to Great Britain and Hitler's last Foreign Minister (the first to be hanged, at 1.02 a.m. on 16 Oct 1946)

2   Field Marshal Wilhelm von Keitel, 64, who had ordered the killing of 50 Allied air force officers after the Great Escape

3   General Ernst Kaltenbrunner, 44, SS and Gestapo leader

4   Reichminister Alfred Rosenberg, 53, ex-Minister for Occupied Eastern Territories

5   Reichminister Hans Frank, 46, ex-Governor of Poland

6   Reichminister Wilhelm Frick, 69, former Minister of the Interior

7   Gauleiter Julius Streicher, 61, editor of anti-Semitic magazine *Die Stürmer*

8   Reichminister Fritz Sauckel, 52, ex-General Plenipotentiary for the Utilization of Labour (the slave-labour programme)

9   Colonel-General Alfred Jodl, 56, former Chief of the General Staff

10 Gauleiter Artur von Seyss-Inquart, 53, Governor of Austria and later Commissioner for Occupied Holland (the last to be hanged)

The International Military Tribunal trials (20 November 1945 to 31 August 1946) sentenced 12 to death. Martin Bormann had escaped and Hermann Goering committed suicide, but the remaining were hanged at Nuremberg Prison on 16 October 1946.

MOST POPULATED COUNTRIES

	Country	Population, estimated 2009
1	China	1,338,612,968
2	India	1,166,079,217
3	USA	306,499,395
4	Indonesia	240,271,522
5	Brazil	193,767,441
6	Pakistan	170,790,583
7	Bangladesh	156,654,645
8	Nigeria	141,617,030
9	Russia	140,041,247
10	Japan	127,078,679
	UK	*61,113,205*
	World	*6,757,062,760*

Source: US Census Bureau, International Data Base

In 2009, the population of Nigeria is set to overtake that of Russia, the only country in the Top 10 whose population is declining. Mexico, with a projected population of 111,211,789, is the only other country with a population of more than 100 million.

LEAST POPULATED COUNTRIES

	Country	Population, estimated 2009
1	Vatican City	557
2	Tuvalu	12,378
3	Nauru	14,014
4	Palau	21,331
5	San Marino	30,324
6	Monaco	32,920
7	Liechtenstein	34,741
8	Saint Kitts and Nevis	39,941
9	Marshall Islands	64,522
10	Antigua and Barbuda	70,194

Source: US Census Bureau, International Data Base

The most recent and unusually precise official statistics published by Vatican City in 2007 revealed that the resident population comprised the Pope and 57 cardinals, 293 clergy members of pontifical representations, 62 other clergy, 101 members of the Swiss Guard and 43 other lay persons. Only those employed by the Holy See can acquire citizenship, which is relinquished when their employment is terminated, but they may then be granted Italian citizenship.

COUNTRIES IN WHICH MEN OUTNUMBER WOMEN

	Country	Estimated men per 100 women, 2009
1	United Arab Emirates	219.5
2	Qatar	182.5
3	Kuwait	153.5
4	Bahrain	124.3
5	Oman	122
6	Saudi Arabia	118
7	Palau	111.6
8	Jordan	110.3
9	Andorra	107.4
10	India	106.3

Source: US Census Bureau, International Data Base

The male/female ratio of the world is balanced virtually 50:50 – in Cameroon, Ecuador, Ghana, Iceland, Indonesia, Mongolia and South Korea precisely so – although in many Western countries male births slightly outnumber female by a very small percentage. There are certain countries, however, where one sex dominates more markedly. There is no definitive explanation of how these imbalances occur, or even whether such apparent differentials represent a true picture. In certain developing countries where births are not accurately recorded and population figures are calculated from census returns, the figures may reflect the numbers of immigrant male workers, or in cultures where women are regarded as second-class citizens and are simply not enumerated.

COUNTRIES IN WHICH WOMEN OUTNUMBER MEN

	Country	Estimated women per 100 men, 2009
1	Estonia	119
2=	Russia	117.6
=	Ukraine	117.6
4	Latvia	116.3
5	Belarus	114.9
6	Lithuania	113.6
7	Armenia	112.4
8	Hungary	111.1
9=	Georgia	109.9
=	Moldova	109.9
=	Monaco	109.9
	UK	*102*
	USA	*104.2*

Source: US Census Bureau, International Data Base

LARGEST COUNTRIES

	Country	Area	Percentage of world total
1	Russia	17,075,200 sq km (6,592,772 sq miles)	**11.5**
2	Canada	9,984,670 sq km (3,855,103 sq miles)	**6.7**
3	USA	9,631,420 sq km (3,718,712 sq miles)	**6.5**
4	China	9,596,960 sq km (3,705,407 sq miles)	**6.4**
5	Brazil	8,511,965 sq km (3,286,488 sq miles)	**5.7**
6	Australia	7,686,850 sq km (2,967,910 sq miles)	**5.2**
7	India	3,287,590 sq km (1,269,346 sq miles)	**2.2**
8	Argentina	2,766,890 sq km (1,068,302 sq miles)	**2.1**
9	Kazakhstan	2,717,300 sq km (1,049,156 sq miles)	**1.9**
10	Sudan	2,505,810 sq km (967,499 sq miles)	**1.7**
	UK	*244,820 sq km (94,526 sq miles)*	*0.2*
	World total	*148,940,000 sq km (57,506,062 sq miles)*	*100*

Source: CIA, *The World Factbook 2007*

This list is based on the total area of a country within its borders, including offshore islands and inland water such as lakes and rivers and reservoirs. It may thus differ from versions in which these are excluded. Antarctica has an approximate area of 13,200,000 sq km (5,096,549 sq miles), but is discounted as it is not considered a country. The countries in the Top 10 collectively comprise 50 per cent of the total Earth's surface.

SMALLEST COUNTRIES

	Country	Area
1	Vatican City	0.44 sq km (0.17 sq miles)
2	Monaco	1.95 sq km (0.75 sq miles)
3	Nauru	21.2 sq km (8.18 sq miles)
4	Tuvalu	25.63 sq km (9.89 sq miles)
5	San Marino	61.2 sq km (23.63 sq miles)
6	Liechtenstein	160 sq km (61.77 sq miles)
7	Marshall Islands	181.43 sq km (70.05 sq miles)
8	Saint Kitts and Nevis	269.4 sq km (104.01 sq miles)
9	Maldives	298 sq km (115.05 sq miles)
10	Malta	315.1 sq km (121.66 sq miles)

There are some 25 'microstates' – independent countries with an area of less than 1,000 sq km (386 sq miles). The 'country' status of the Vatican is questionable, since its government and other features are intricately linked with those of Italy. The Vatican did become part of unified Italy in the 19th century, but its identity as an independent state was recognized by a treaty of 11 February 1929. If it is discounted, Grenada (344 sq km/132.81 sq miles) would join the list.

LONGEST PLACE NAMES*

Name	Letters

1 Krung Thep Mahanakhon Amon Rattanakosin **168**
Mahinthara Ayuthaya Mahadilok Phop Noppharat
Ratchathani Burirom Udomratchaniwet Mahasathan
Amon Piman Awatan Sathit Sakkathattiya Witsanukam
Prasit

It means 'The city of angels, the great city, the eternal jewel city, the impregnable city of God Indra, the grand capital of the world endowed with nine precious gems, the happy city, abounding in an enormous royal palace that resembles the heavenly abode where reigns the reincarnated god, a city given by Indra and built by Vishnukarn'. When the poetic name of Bangkok, capital of Thailand, is used, it is usually abbreviated to 'Krung Thep' (city of angels).

2 Taumatawhakatangihangakoauauotamate-
aturipukakapiki-maungahoronukupokaiwhen-
uakitanatahu **85**

This is the longer version (the other has a mere 83 letters) of the Maori name of a hill in New Zealand. It translates as 'The place where Tamatea, the man with the big knees, who slid, climbed and swallowed mountains, known as land-eater, played on the flute to his loved one'.

3 Gorsafawddachaidraigddanheddogle-
ddollônpenrhyn-areurdraethceredigion **67**

A name contrived by the Fairbourne Steam Railway, Gwynedd, North Wales, for publicity purposes and in order to outdo its rival, No. 4. It means 'The Mawddach station and its dragon teeth at the Northern Penrhyn Road on the golden beach of Cardigan Bay'.

4 Llanfairpwllgwyngyllgogerychwyrndrob-
wllllantysilio-gogogoch **58**

This is the place in Gwynedd famed especially for the length of its railway tickets. It means 'St Mary's Church in the hollow of the white hazel near to the rapid whirlpool of the church of St Tysilo near the Red Cave'. Questions have been raised about its authenticity, since its official name comprises only the first 20 letters and the full name appears to have been invented as a hoax in the 19th century by a local tailor.

5   El Pueblo de Nuestra Señora la Reina de los Ángeles   **57**
     de la Porciúncula

The site of a Franciscan mission and the full Spanish name of Los Angeles, it means 'The town of Our Lady the Queen of the Angels of the Little Portion'. Nowadays it is customarily known by its initial letters, LA, making it also one of the shortest-named cities in the world.

6   Chargoggagoggmanchaugagoggchaubunagungamaug   **43**

America's longest place name, a lake near Webster, Massachusetts. Its Indian name, loosely translated, is claimed to mean 'You fish on your side, I'll fish on mine, and no one fishes in the middle'. It is said to be pronounced 'Char-gogg-a-gogg [pause] man-chaug-a-gogg [pause] chau-bun-a-gung-a-maug'. It is, however, an invented extension of its real name (Chaubunagungamaug or 'boundary fishing place'), devised in the 1920s by Larry Daly, the editor of the *Webster Times*.

7=   Lower North Branch Little Southwest Miramichi   **40**

Canada's longest place name – a short river in New Brunswick.

=   Villa Real de la Santa Fé de San Francisco   **40**
     de Asis

The full Spanish name of Santa Fe, New Mexico, translates as 'Royal city of the holy faith of St Francis of Assisi'.

9   Te Whakatakanga-o-te-ngarehu-o-te-ahi-a-Tamatea   **38**

The Maori name of Hammer Springs, New Zealand. Like No. 2 in this list, it refers to a legend of Tamatea, explaining how the springs were warmed by 'the falling of the cinders of the fire of Tamatea'. Its name is variously written either hyphenated or as a single word.

10   Meallan Liath Coire Mhic Dhubhghaill   **32**

The longest multiple name in Scotland, a place near Aultanrynie, Highland, alternatively spelled Meallan Liath Coire Mhic Dhughaill (30 letters).

* Including single-word, hyphenated and multiple names

TOP 10
LONGEST PLACE NAMES IN THE UK*

	Name/location	Letters
1	Gorsafawddachaidraigddanheddogle-ddollônpenrhyn-areurdraethceredigion (see Top 10 longest place names, No. 3)	67
2	Llanfairpwllgwyngyllgogerychwyrndrob-wllllantysilio-gogogoch (see Top 10 longest place names, No. 4)	58
3	Sutton-under-Whitestonecliffe, North Yorkshire	27
4	Llansantffraid-ym-mechain, Powys	23
5	Llanfihangel-yng-Ngwynfa, Powys	22
6=	Llanfihangel-y-Creuddyn, Ceredigion	21
=	Llanfihangel-y-traethau, Gwynedd	21
8	Cottonshopeburnfoot, Northumberland	19
9=	Blakehopeburnhaugh, Northumberland	18
=	Coignafeuinternich, Highland	18

* Single and hyphenated only

Runners-up include Claddach-baleshare and Claddach-knockline, both in North Uist, Outer Hebrides, each having 17 letters. Next come Combeinteignhead, Doddiscombsleigh, Moretonhampstead, Stokeinteignhead and Woolfardisworthy (pronounced 'Woolsery'), all of which are in Devon and have 16 letters. The longest multiple name in England is North Leverton with Habblesthorpe, Nottinghamshire (30 letters), followed by Sulhampstead Bannister Upper End, West Berkshire (29). In Wales it is Lower Llanfihangel-y-Creuddyn, Ceredigion (26), followed by Llansantffraed Cwmdeuddwr, Powys (24), and in Scotland Meallan Liath Coire Mhic Dhubhghaill, Highland (32), Loch Airidh Mhic Fhionnlaidh Dhuibh (31), a loch on the island of Lewis, and Huntingtower and Ruthvenfield, Perth and Kinross (27). If the parameters are extended to encompass Ireland, the single-words Castletownconyersmaceniery (26), County Limerick, and Muickeenachidirdhashaile (24) and Muckanaghederdauhalia (21), both in County Galway, are scooped into the net. The shortest place name in the UK is Ae in Dumfries and Galloway, Scotland. There are numerous three-letter British place names, among them Bix, Cog, three Eyes (or rather, three places called Eye), Ham, Hey, Hoe, How, Hoy, Hoo, Ide, Nax and Wig, with Ham (17 examples) being the commonest.

MOST COMMON STREET NAMES IN THE UK

1 High Street
2 Station Road
3 Main Street
4 Park Road
5 Church Road
6 Church Street
7 London Road
8 Victoria Road
9 Green Lane
10 Manor Road

Source: HBOS

TALLEST HABITABLE BUILDINGS

	Building/location	Year completed	Storeys	Roof height
1	Burj Dubai, Dubai, UAR	2008*	162	643.2 m (2,110 ft)
2	Shanghai World Financial Center, Shanghai, China	2008*	101	492 m (1,614 ft)
3	Abraj Al Bait Hotel Tower, Mecca, Saudi Arabia	2008*	76	485 m (1,591 ft)
4	Greenland Square Zifeng Tower, Nanjing, China	2008*	69	450 m (1,476 ft)
5	Taipei 101, Taipei, Taiwan	2004	101	449.2 m (1,474 ft)
6	Sears Tower, Chicago, USA	1973	110	442.3 m (1,451 ft)
7	Guangzhou Twin Towers, Guangzhou, China	2009*	103	437.5 m (1,435 ft)
8	Jin Mao Tower, Shanghai, China	1998	88	420.5 m (1,380 ft)
9	Princess Tower, Dubai, UAE	2009*	107	414 m (1,358 ft)
10	Al Hamra Tower, Kuwait	2008*	77	412 m (1,352 ft)

* Under construction, scheduled completion date

TALLEST HABITABLE BUILDINGS IN THE UK*

	Building/location	Year completed	Storeys	Roof height
1	One Canada Square, Canary Wharf, London	1991	50	**235.1 m** (771 ft)
2=	8 Canada Square (HSBC Tower), Canary Wharf, London	2002	45	**199.5 m** (655 ft)
=	25 Canada Square, Canary Wharf, London	2001	45	**199.5 m** (655 ft)
4	Tower 42 (formerly National Westminster Tower), London	1980	47	**183 m** (600 ft)
5	30 St Mary Axe ('The Gherkin'), London	2004	41	**179.8 m** (590 ft)
6	Broadgate Tower, London	2008	36	**164.3 m** (539 ft)
7	Beetham Tower, Manchester	2006	50	**157 m** (515 ft)
8	1 Churchill Place, London	2004	32	**156.4 m** (513 ft)
9=	25 Bank Street, London	2003	33	**153 m** (502 ft)
=	40 Bank Street, London	2003	33	**153 m** (502 ft)

* Excluding communications masts and towers, chimneys and church spires

LONGEST SUSPENSION BRIDGES

	Bridge/location	Year completed	Length of main span
1	Akashi-Kaikyo, Kobe-Naruto, Japan	1998	**1,991 m (6,532 ft)**
2	Xihoumen, China	2007	**1,650 m (5,413 ft)**
3	Great Belt, Denmark	1997	**1,624 m (5,328 ft)**
4	Ryungyang, China	2005	**1,490 m (4,888 ft)**
5	Humber Estuary, UK	1980	**1,410 m (4,625 ft)**
6	Jiangyin, China	1998	**1,385 m (4,543 ft)**
7	Tsing Ma, Hong Kong, China	1997	**1,377 m (4,518 ft)**
8	Verrazano Narrows, New York, USA	1964	**1,298 m (4,260 ft)**
9=	Golden Gate, San Francisco, USA	1937	**1,280 m (4,200 ft)**
=	Yangluo, China	2007	**1,280 m (4,200 ft)**

The planned Messina Strait Bridge between Sicily and Calabria, Italy, would have had the longest centre span of any bridge at 3,300 m (10,827 ft), but the project was cancelled on 11 October 2006.

LONGEST RAIL TUNNELS

	Tunnel/location	Year completed	Length
1	AlpTransit Gotthard, Switzerland	2018*	57,072 m (187,244 ft)
2	Seikan, Japan	1988	53,850 m (176,673 ft)
3	Channel Tunnel, France/England	1994	50,450 m (165,518 ft)
4	Moscow Metro (Serpukhovsko–Timiryazevskaya line), Russia	1983	38,900 m (127,625 ft)
5	Lötschberg Base, Switzerland	2007	34,577 m (113,442 ft)
6	Guadarrama, Spain	2007	28,377 m (97,100 ft)
7	London Underground (East Finchley–Morden, Northern Line), UK	1939	27,840 m (91,339 ft)
8	Hakkoda, Japan	2010*	26,455 m (86,795 ft)
9	Iwate-Ichinohe, Japan	2002	25,810 m (84,678 ft)
10	Pajares Base, Spain	2011*	24,667 m (80,928 ft)

* Under construction, scheduled completion date

LONGEST ROAD TUNNELS

	Tunnel/location	Year completed	Length
1	Lærdal, Norway	2000	24,510 m (80,413 ft)
2	Zhongnanshan, China	2007	18,040 m (59,186 ft)
3	St Gotthard, Switzerland	1980	16,918 m (55,505 ft)
4	Arlberg, Austria	1978	13,972 m (45,850 ft)
5	Hsuehshan, Taiwan	2006	12,900 m (42,323 ft)
6	Fréjus, France/Italy	1980	12,895 m (42,306 ft)
7	Mont-Blanc, France/Italy	1965	11,611 m (38,094 ft)
8	Gudvangen, Norway	1991	11,428 m (37,493 ft)
9	Folgefonn, Norway	2001	11,100 m (36,417 ft)
10	Kan-Etsu II (southbound), Japan	1991	11,010 m (36,122 ft)

ONLINE LANGUAGES

	Language	Percentage of all internet users	Internet users*
1	English	30.1	379,529,347
2	Chinese (Mandarin)	14.7	184,901,513
3	Spanish	9	113,463,158
4	Japanese	6.9	87,540,000
5	French	5.1	63,761,141
6	German	4.9	61,912,361
7	Portuguese	4	50,828,760
8	Arabic	3.7	46,359,140
9	Korean	2.7	34,430,000
10	Italian	2.6	33,143,152
	Top 10 languages	*83.7*	*1,055,868,572*
	Rest of world languages	*16.3*	*206,164,125*
	World total	*100*	*1,262,032,697*

* As at 30 November 2007
Source: www.internetworldstats.com

MOST-SPOKEN LANGUAGES*

	Language	Speakers
1	Chinese (Mandarin)	873,014,298
2	Spanish	322,299,171
3	English	309,352,280
4	Hindi	180,764,791
5	Portuguese	177,457,180
6	Bengali	171,070,202
7	Russian	145,031,551
8	Japanese	122,433,899
9	German	95,392,978
10	Chinese (Wu)	77,175,000

* Primary speakers only
Source: Raymond G. Gordon Jr (ed.), *Ethnologue: Languages of the World*, 15th edition (Dallas, Texas: SIL International, 2005). Online version: www.ethnologue.com.

LONGEST WORDS IN THE *OXFORD ENGLISH DICTIONARY*

	Word/earliest recorded use	Letters
1	Supercalifragilisticexpialidocious, 1964	34
	Meaning 'wonderful', from song of this title in the film *Mary Poppins*.	
2	Floccinaucinihilipilification, 1741	29
	Meaning 'the action or habit of estimating as worthless'.	
3	Honorificabilitudinitatibus, 1599	27
	Meaning 'honourableness'.	
4	Antidisestablishmentarians, 1900	26
	Meaning 'those opposed to the disestablishment of the Church of England'.	
5	Overintellectualization, 1922	23
	Meaning 'excessive intellectualization'.	
6=	Incircumscriptibleness, 1550	22
	Meaning 'incapable of being circumscribed'.	
=	Omnirepresentativeness, 1842	22
	Meaning 'the quality of being representative of all forms or kinds'.	
=	Reinstitutionalization, 1978	22
	Meaning 'institutionalize again'.	
9	Undercharacterization, 1968	21
	Meaning to depict or play with insufficient characterization or subtlety.	
10	Lithochromatographic, 1843	20
	Colour printing technique using stone.	

These are strictly non-medical terms or names of chemical compounds, which can achieve lengths running into thousands of letters.

OLDEST UNIVERSITIES IN THE UK

	University	Founded
1	Oxford	1117
2	Cambridge	1209
3	St Andrews	1411
4	Glasgow	1451
5	Aberdeen	1495
6	Edinburgh	1583
7	Dublin*	1592
8	Durham†	1832
9	London‡	1836
10	Manchester	1851

* Ireland was not then a separate country
† A short-lived Cromwellian establishment was set up in 1657
‡ Constituent colleges founded earlier: University College 1826, King's College 1828

Although its constituent colleges were founded earlier – Lampeter 1822, Aberystwyth 1872, Cardiff 1883, Bangor 1884 – the University of Wales dates from 1893.

TOP 10
BESTSELLING NOVELS

	Book/first published	Minimum estimated sales*
1	J. K. Rowling, *Harry Potter and the Philosopher's Stone*, 1997	120,000,000
2	Agatha Christie, *And Then There Were None*, 1939	115,000,000
3	J. R. R. Tolkien, *The Lord of the Rings*, 1954–5	100,000,000
4	J. K. Rowling, *Harry Potter and the Chamber of Secrets*, 1998	77,000,000
5	J. K. Rowling, *Harry Potter and the Goblet of Fire*, 2000	66,000,000
6=	J. K. Rowling, *Harry Potter and the Half-Blood Prince*, 2005	65,000,000
=	J. D. Salinger, *The Catcher in the Rye*, 1951	65,000,000
8	Dan Brown, *The Da Vinci Code*, 2003	64,000,000
9	J. K. Rowling, *Harry Potter and the Prisoner of Azkaban*, 1999	60,000,000
10	J. K. Rowling, *Harry Potter and the Order of the Phoenix*, 2003	58,000,000

* Including translations

LATEST 'ODDEST TITLE OF THE YEAR' COMPETITION WINNERS

2006   *The Stray Shopping Carts of Eastern North America: A Guide to Field Identification*

2005   *People Who Don't Know They're Dead: How They Attach Themselves to Unsuspecting Bystanders and What to Do About It*

2004   *Bombproof Your Horse*

2003   *The Big Book of Lesbian Horse Stories*

2002   *Living with Crazy Buttocks*

2001   *Butterworths Corporate Manslaughter Service*

2000   *High Performance Stiffened Structures*

1999   *Weeds in a Changing World*

1998   *Developments in Dairy Cow Breeding and Management: And New Opportunities to Widen the Uses of Straw*

1997   *The Joy of Sex: Pocket Edition*

Every year since 1978 the Diagram Group and the *Bookseller* have organized a competition for the book title that 'most outrageously exceeds all bounds of credibility'. In 1987 and 1991 the judges did not consider that the standard was sufficiently high, so no award was presented. In other years, however, many of the runners-up were as extraordinary as the winning entries, among them: *Entertaining with Insects: The Original Guide to Insect Cookery*; *Scurvy Past and Present*; *Big and Very Big Hole Drilling*; *The Potatoes of Bolivia: Their Breeding, Value and Evolutionary Relationship*; *The Social History of Gas Masks and Knifethrowing: A Practical Guide*.

INTERNET SEARCH WORDS

1   sex
2   porn
3   MySpace
4   youporn
5   google
6   eBay
7   yahoo
8   pussy
9   YouTube
10 hentai (Japanese porn)

Source: Wordtracker, based on a survey of 313,168,488 search terms

INTERNET SEARCH SUBJECTS

1   Poker

2   MySpace

3   Britney Spears

4   Paris Hilton

5   Golf

6   YouTube

7   Naruto (manga series)

8   Disney

9   Pokemon

10 WWE (World Wrestling Entertainment)

Source: Lycos 500™

The Lycos 500™ has monitored the most popular people, places and things Lycos users search for during the past eight years. In 2007, Poker occupied its No.1 slot for the second year running.

OLDEST NEWSPAPERS

	Newspaper	Country	Founded
1	*Haarlems Dagblad*	Netherlands	1656
2	*Gazzetta di Mantova*	Italy	1664
3	*London Gazette*	UK	1665
4	*Wiener Zeitung*	Austria	1703
5	*Hildesheimer Allgemeine Zeitung*	Germany	1705
6	*Berrow's Worcester Journal*	UK	1709
7	*Newcastle Journal*	UK	1711
8	*Stamford Mercury*	UK	1712
9	*Northampton Mercury*	UK	1720
10	*Hanauer Anzeiger*	Germany	1725

This list includes only newspapers that have been published continuously since their founding under the same name – or at least containing the name, as in the case of the *Worcester Journal*, which was founded in 1690 as *Worcester Post Man*, published irregularly until it became the *Worcester Journal* in 1709, then adopted the name of its proprietor, Harvey Berrow, to become *Berrow's Worcester Journal* in 1753. The former No.1 on this list, the Swedish *Post- och Inrikes Tidningar*, founded in 1645, ceased publication on paper on 1 January 2007 and is now available only online.

DAILY NEWSPAPERS IN THE UK

	Newspaper	Average net circulation*
1	*Sun*	3,209,776
2	*Daily Mail*	2,313,908
3	*Mirror*	1,906,347
4	*Daily Telegraph*	890,086
5	*Daily Express*	752,702
6	*Daily Star*	722,969
7	*The Times*	633,718
8	*Financial Times*	452,448
9	*Daily Record*	393,788
10	*Guardian*	378,394

* January 2008
Source: Audit Bureau of Circulations Ltd

SUNDAY NEWSPAPERS IN THE UK

	Newspaper	Average net circulation*
1	*News of the World*	3,264,676
2	*Mail on Sunday*	2,330,366
3	*Sunday Mirror*	1,366,922
4	*Sunday Times*	1,231,374
5	*Sunday Express*	704,436
6	*People*	669,362
7	*Sunday Telegraph*	633,639
8	*Sunday Mail* (Scotland)	487,975
9	*The Observer*	444,951
10	*Sunday Post* (Scotland)	412,037

* January 2008
Source: Audit Bureau of Circulations Ltd

MAGAZINES

	Magazine	Country	Average net circulation
1	*Reader's Digest*	USA	12,078,000
2	*Better Homes and Gardens*	USA	7,605,000
3	*Family Circle*	USA	4,634,000
4	*Women's Day*	USA	4,205,000
5	*Time*	USA	4,112,000
6	*Ladies' Home Journal*	USA	4,101,000
7	*Kampioen*	Netherlands	3,756,000
8	*People*	USA	3,625,000
9	*Playboy*	USA	3,215,000
10	*Newsweek*	USA	3,183,000

Source: International Federation of Audit Bureaux of Circulations

MAGAZINES IN THE UK

	Title	Average net circulation*
1	*What's on TV*	1,404,950
2	*TV Choice*	1,386,900
3	*Radio Times*	1,038,914
4	*Take a Break*	1,001,003
5	*Saga Magazine*	651,096
6	*Reader's Digest*	628,389
7	*OK! Magazine*	607,405
8	*Glamour*	550,016
9	*Closer*	548,594
10	*Heat*	533,034

* Actively purchased July–December 2007
Source: Audit Bureau of Circulations Ltd

MEN'S MAGAZINES IN THE UK

	Magazine	Circulation*
1	*Sport*	317,209
2	*FHM*	315,149
3	*Nuts*	270,053
4	*Men's Health*	226,682
5	*Zoo*	179,006
6	*GQ*	117,796
7	*Loaded*	115,065
8	*Stuff*	96,655
9	*Maxim*	78,456
10	*Men's Fitness*	65,502

* Per issue average 1 July–31 December 2007
Source: Audit Bureau of Circulations Ltd

MOST VALUABLE BRITISH COMICS

	Comic/issue no.	Date	Value*
1	*Dandy*, 1	4 Dec 1937	£20,350
2	*Beano*, 1	30 Jul 1938	£12,100
3	*Dandy*, 2	11 Dec 1937	£7,500
4	*Beano*, 2	6 Aug 1938	£3,000
5	*The Magic Comic*, 1	22 Jul 1939	£1,500
6	*Eagle*, 1	14 Apr 1950	£1,125
7	*Viz*, 1	Dec 1979	£950
8	*Topper*, 1	7 Dec 1953	£369
9	*Commando*, 1	Jul 1961	£375
10	*Beezer*, 1	21 Jan 1956	£300

* Based on estimates and auction records; to prevent the entire list being dominated by *Dandy* and *Beano*, only the first two issues of each are included

MOST VALUABLE AMERICAN COMICS

Comic/publisher	Value*
1 *Action Comics*, No. 1 (DC)	**$2,320,000**
Published in June 1938, the first issue of Action Comics marked the original appearance of Superman.	
2= *Detective Comics*, No. 27 (DC)	**$1,600,000**
Issued in May 1939, it is prized as the first comic book to feature Batman.	
= *Superman*, No. 1 (DC)	**$1,600,000**
The first comic book devoted to Superman, published in Summer 1939.	
4 *All American Comics*, No. 16 (All American)	**$800,000**
The Green Lantern made his debut in the issue dated July 1940.	
5= *Detective Comics*, No.1 (DC)	**$672,000**
Isued in March 1937, this was an anthology that featured detective Slam Bradley.	
= *Marvel Comics*, No. 1 (Marvel)	**$672,000**
The Human Torch was first introduced in the October 1939 issue.	
7 *Batman*, No. 1 (DC)	**$640,000**
Published in Spring 1940, this was the first comic book devoted to Batman.	
8 *Captain America Comics*, No. 1 (Timely)	**$512,000**
The February 1935 issue was the first containing material that had not previously appeared in newspapers.	
9 *Flash Comics*, No. 1 (DC)	**$368,000**
Dated January 1940, and featuring The Flash, it is rare because it was produced in small numbers for promotional purposes.	
10 *More Fun Comics*, No. 52 (DC)	**$288,000**
The Spectre made his debut in the issue dated February 1940.	

* For example in 'Mint' condition

MOST EXPENSIVE ITEMS OF ROCK MEMORABILIA SOLD AT AUCTION

	Item/auction	Price*
1	John Lennon's 1965 Rolls-Royce Phantom V touring limousine, Sotheby's, New York, 29 Jun 1985	£1,768,462
2	John Lennon's Steinway Model Z upright piano, Fleetwood-Owen online auction, Hard Rock Café, London and New York, 17 Oct 2000	£1,450,000
3	Jerry Garcia's 'Tiger' guitar, Guernsey's at Studio 54, New York, 8 May 2002	£657,850
4	Jerry Garcia's 'Wolf' guitar, Guernsey's at Studio 54, New York, 8 May 2002	£542,425
5	Eric Clapton's 1956–7 'Blackie' Fender Stratocaster, Christie's, New York, 25 Jun 2004	527,918
6	Eric Clapton's 1964 Gibson acoustic ES-335, Christie's, New York, 25 Jun 2004	£465,659
7	Eric Clapton's 1939 Martin acoustic, Christie's, New York, 25 Jun 2004	£434,890
8	Stevie Ray Vaughan's/Eric Clapton's 'Lenny' Fender Stratocaster, Christie's, New York, 25 Jun 2004	£342,582

| 9 | Eric Clapton's 'Brownie' Fender Stratocaster, Christie's, New York, 24 Jun 1999 | **£313,425** |
| 10 | George Harrison's 1964 Gibson SG, Christie's, New York, 17 Dec 2004 | **£294,041** |

* Including buyer's premium, where appropriate

Pioneered particularly by Sotheby's in London, rock and pop memorabilia has become big business – especially if it involves personal association with mega-stars such as the Beatles. The painted bass drumskin that appears on the album sleeve of *Sgt. Pepper's Lonely Hearts Club Band* made £52,100 in 1994, and in the same year a reel-to-reel tape recording of 16-year-old John Lennon singing with the Quarrymen at a church fête in Liverpool on 6 July 1957 realized £78,500, while a single page of Lennon's lyrics for 'I Am The Walrus' fetched the same amount in 1999. In 2003, £269,526 was paid for Lennon's handwritten lyrics for 'Nowhere Man'. Bernie Taupin's lyrics for the rewritten 'Candle in the Wind', sung by Elton John at the funeral of Princess Diana, was sold for £278,512 at a charity auction in 1998. Iconic guitars dominate the list, however, with prices almost as high as those in the Top 10 being paid for instruments once owned by Bill Haley, Buddy Holly, Elvis Presley and Paul McCartney. The Fender Stratocaster played by Jimi Hendrix at the Woodstock Festival in 1969 was sold at auction in 1990 for £174,000, but later changed hands privately for £750,000 before being acquired by Microsoft co-founder Paul Allen for an undisclosed – but presumably even higher – amount.

MOST EXPENSIVE ITEMS OF FILM MEMORABILIA SOLD AT AUCTION

	Item/auction	Price
1	Marilyn Monroe's beaded dress, worn 19 May 1962 , when she sang 'Happy Birthday Mr President' to John F. Kennedy, Christie's, New York, 27 Oct 1999	**£767,735**
2	Audrey Hepburn's black dress from *Breakfast at Tiffany's* (1961), Christie's, London, 5 Dec 2006	**£467,000**
3	Judy Garland's ruby slippers from *The Wizard of Oz* (1939), Christie's, New York, 26 May 2000	**£410,874**
4	Marilyn Monroe's piano, Christie's, New York, 27 Oct 1999	**£401,078**
5	Vivien Leigh's Oscar for *Gone with the Wind* (1939), Sotheby's, New York, 15 Dec 1993	**£380,743**
6	Clark Gable's Oscar for *It Happened One Night* (1934), Christie's, Los Angeles, 15 Dec 1996	**£364,500**
7	Statue of the Maltese Falcon from *The Maltese Falcon* (1941), Christie's Rockefeller, New York, 5 Dec 1994	**£255,580**

8	Poster for *The Mummy* (1932), Sotheby's, New York, 1 Mar 1997	£252,109
9	Poster for *Metropolis* (1927), Sotheby's, New York, 28 Oct 2000	£246,067
10	James Bond's Aston Martin DB5 from *Goldfinger* (1964), Sotheby's, New York, 28 Jun 1986	£179,793

This list encompasses memorabilia related to films and film stars, but excludes animated film celluloids or 'cels' – the individually painted scenes that are shot in sequence to make up cartoon films. Among near-misses in the £100,000-plus league are Marlon Brando's script for *The Godfather* (1972), which made £173,373 in 2005, James Bond's Aston Martin DB5 from *GoldenEye* (1995), sold for £157,750 in 2001, Clark Gable's script for *Gone with the Wind*, which achieved £146,700 in 1996, the 'Rosebud' sledge from *Citizen Kane* (1941), £140,000 in 1996, and Herman J. Mankiewicz's scripts for this film and an earlier draft (originally called American), £139,157 in 1989. Oscar statuettes are occasionally auctioned, but since 1950, to prevent them from becoming collectables, winners have signed agreements that prohibit their sale, except back to the Academy of Motion Picture Arts and Sciences – for one dollar. The Oscar awarded to Clark Gable at No. 6 in the Top 10, was purchased by Steven Spielberg and returned to the Academy, as he did again in 2001 with Bette Davis's Oscar for *Jezebel* (1938). In 2007, Orson Welles's Oscar for *Citizen Kane*, with a pre-sale estimate of $1.2 million, failed to find a buyer at auction.

MOST EXPENSIVE PAINTINGS BY BRITISH ARTISTS SOLD AT AUCTION

	Painting/artist	Auction	Price
1	*Study from Innocent X*, Francis Bacon	Sotheby's, New York, 15 May 2007	£26,583,773
2	*Triptych*, Francis Bacon	Christie's, London 6 Feb 2008	£26,340,500
3	*Study of a Bullfight No.1*, Francis Bacon	Sotheby's, New York, 14 Nov 2007	£22,257,790
4	*Self-portrait*, Francis Bacon	Sotheby's, London 21 Jun 2007	£21,580,000
5	*Giudecca, La Donna della Salute and San Giorgio*, J M W Turner	Christie's, New York, 6 Apr 2006	£20,439,038
6	*Study for portrait II*, Francis Bacon	Christie's, London, 8 Feb 2007	£14,020,000
7	*Group with Parasols*, John Singer Sargent	Sotheby's, New York, 1 Dec 2004	£12,311,879
8	*The Lock*, John Constable	Sotheby's, London, 14 Nov 1990	£10,780,000
9	*Portrait of Omai*, Sir Joshua Reynolds	Sotheby's, London, 29 Nov 2001	£10,343,500
10	*Seated Woman*, Francis Bacon	Sotheby's, Paris, 12 Dec 2007	£9,847,467

MOST EXPENSIVE PAINTINGS SOLD AT AUCTION

	Painting/artist	Auction	Price
1	*Garçon à la pipe*, Pablo Picasso	Sotheby's, New York, 5 May 2004	£54,782,014
2	*Dora Maar au chat*, Pablo Picasso	Sotheby's, New York, 3 May 2006	£52,017,526
3	*The Massacre of the of the Innocents*, Sir Peter Paul Rubens	Sotheby's, London, 10 Jul 2002	£49,506,648
4	*Portrait du Dr Gachet*, Vincent van Gogh	Christie's, New, York, 15 May 1990	£49,005,049
5	*Bal au Moulin de la Galette, Montmartre*, Pierre-Auguste Renoir	Sotheby's, New, York, 17 May 1990	£46,501,935
6	*Portrait of Adele Bloch-Bauer II*, Gustav Klimt	Christie's, New York, 8 Nov 2006	£46,193,851
7	*Portrait de l'Artiste Sans Barbe*, Vincent van Gogh	Christie's, New York, 19 Nov 1998	£42,856,925
8	*Femme aux Bras Croises*, Pablo Picasso	Christie's, New York, 8 Nov 2000	£38,364,859
9	*Rideau, Cruchon et Compôtier*, Paul Cézanne	Sotheby's, New York, 10 May 1999	£37,191,113
10	*Irises*, Vincent van Gogh	Sotheby's, New York, 11 Nov 1987	£30,179,171

TOP 10

MOST EXPENSIVE CARS SOLD AT AUCTION

	Car/auction*	Price
1	1962 Ferrari GTO, Sotheby's, Monte Carlo, 21 May 1990	£6,389,398
2	1931 Bugatti Royale, Type 41 Chassis '41.141', Christie's, London (at the Royal Albert Hall), 19 Nov 1987	£5,500,000
3	1962 Ferrari 330 TRI/LM Testa Rossa, RM Auctions, Maranello, Italy, 20 May 2007	£4,705,938
4	1929 Bugatti Royale, Chassis '41.150', Kruse (William F. Harrah Collection Sale), Reno, USA, 15 Jun 1986	£4,267,892
5	1929 Mercedes-Benz 38/250 SSK, Bonham's, Chichester, 3 Sep 2004	£4,180,000
6	1937 Mercedes-Benz 540K Special Roadster, RM Auctions, London, 31 Oct 2007	£3,967,125
7	1966 Ferrari 330 P3, Christie's, Pebble Beach, California, USA, 19 Aug 2000	£3,772,926
8	1904 Rolls-Royce 10hp two-seater, Bonhams, Olympia, London, 3 Dec 2007	£3,521.500
9	1958 Ferrari 412S, RM Auctions, Monterey, California, USA, 18 Aug 2006	£2,961,063
10	1953 Ferrari 340/375 MM Competizione, RM Auctions, Maranello, Italy, 20 May 2007	£2,874,900

* Where the same car has subsequently been re-auctioned and fetched a lower price, only the highest is listed

SINGLES OF ALL TIME

	Title/artist/group	Year	Sales exceed
1	'Candle in the Wind'/ Something about the Way You Look Tonight', Elton John	1997	**37,000,000**
2	'White Christmas', Bing Crosby	1942	**30,000,000**
3	'Rock Around the Clock', Bill Haley and His Comets	1954	**17,000,000**
4	'I Want to Hold Your Hand', The Beatles	1963	**12,000,000**
5=	'It's Now or Never', Elvis Presley	1960	**10,000,00**
=	'Hey Jude', The Beatles	1968	**10,000,000**
=	'I Will Always Love You', Whitney Houston	1992	**10,000,000**
8=	'Diana', Paul Anka	1957	**9,000,000**
=	'Hound Dog'/'Don't Be Cruel', Elvis Presley	1956	**9,000,000**
10=	'(Everything I Do) I Do It for You', Bryan Adams	1991	**8,000,000**
=	'I'm a Believer', The Monkees	1966	**8,000,000**

Source: Music Information Database

SINGLES OF ALL TIME IN THE UK

	Title/artist/group	Year	Estimated sales
1	'Candle in the Wind'/ 'Something About the Way You Look Tonight', Elton John	1997	4,864,611
2	'Do They Know It's Christmas?', Band Aid	1984	3,550,000
3	'Bohemian Rhapsody', Queen	1975/91	2,130,000
4	'Mull of Kintyre', Wings	1977	2,050,000
5	'Rivers of Babylon'/'Brown Girl in the Ring', Boney M	1978	1,985,000
6	'You're the One that I Want', John Travolta and Olivia Newton-John	1978	1,975,000
7	'Relax', Frankie Goes to Hollywood	1984	1,910,000
8	'She Loves You', The Beatles	1963	1,890,000
9	'Unchained Melody', Robson Green and Jerome Flynn	1995	1,843,701
10	'Mary's Boy Child'/'Oh My Lord', Boney M	1978	1,790,000

Source: The Official UK Charts Company

Some 80 singles have sold over 1 million copies each in the UK during the last 50 years, these being the 10 at the head of the elite field. Both the Band Aid single and the version of 'Candle in the Wind' for Princess Diana's funeral achieved their remarkable sales as by-products of two exceptional events.

ALBUMS OF ALL TIME

	Artist/album/year	Sales (millions) USA	World total
1	Michael Jackson, *Thriller* (1982)	27	**104**
2=	Eagles, *Their Greatest Hits 1971–1975* (1976)	29	**42**
=	AC/DC, *Back in Black* (1980)	21	**42**
=	*The Bodyguard* (soundtrack) (1992)	17	**42**
5=	Pink Floyd, *The Dark Side of the Moon* (1973)	15	**40**
=	*Saturday Night Fever* (soundtrack) (1977)	15	**40**
=	Back Street Boys, *Millennium* (1999)	13	**40**
8	Shania Twain, *Come On Over* (1997)	20	**39**
9	Meat Loaf, *Bat Out of Hell* (1978)	14	**37**
10=	The Beatles, *Sgt. Pepper's Lonely Hearts Club Band* (1967)	11	**32**
=	Led Zeppelin, *Led Zeppelin IV* (1971)	23	**32**
=	*Dirty Dancing* (soundtrack) (1987)	11	**32**

TOP 10
ALBUMS IN THE UK

	Title/artist/group/year	Sales
1	*Greatest Hits*, Queen (1981)	5,407,587
2	*Sgt. Pepper's Lonely Hearts Club Band*, The Beatles (1967)	4,803,292
3	*(What's the Story) Morning Glory*, Oasis (1995)	4,303,504
4	*Brothers in Arms*, Dire Straits (1985)	3,946,931
5	*Abba Gold Greatest Hits*, Abba (1990)	3,932,316
6	*The Dark Side of the Moon*, Pink Floyd (1973)	3,759,958
7	*Greatest Hits II*, Queen (1991)	3,631,321
8	*Thriller*, Michael Jackson (1982)	3,570,250
9	*Bad*, Michael Jackson (1987)	3,549,950
10	*The Immaculate Collection*, Madonna (1990)	3,364,785

Source: The Official UK Charts Company

Recent research has shown Queen's *Greatest Hits* album to have overtaken long-standing list-leader *Sgt. Pepper's Lonely Hearts Club Band*. The latter album was both a commercial success and a critical triumph, considered by many as the most influential rock album ever and hailed by *Rolling Stone* magazine as 'the greatest album of all time'. It is, however, the only record on this list that has never received a BPI (British Phonographic Industry) award, since most of its sales occurred prior to the adoption of Gold and Platinum awards in 1973.

FIRST DANCE SONG REQUESTS AT WEDDINGS IN THE UK

1   'I Cross My Heart', George Strait
2   'I Swear', John M. Montgomery/All 4 One
3   'I Can Love You Like That', John M. Montgomery
4   'I'll Be There', Mariah Carey
5   '(Everything I Do) I Do It for You', Bryan Adams
6   'Don't Know Much', Linda Ronstadt and Aaron Neville
7   'All My Life', Linda Ronstadt and Aaron Neville
8   'Unchained Melody', Righteous Brothers
9   'A Whole New World', Peabo Bryson and Regina Belle
10 'No Ordinary Love', Sade

Source: Sound Connection

SONGS REQUESTED AT FUNERALS

1 'Goodbye My Lover', James Blunt
2 'Angels', Robbie Williams
3 'I've Had the Time of My Life', Jennifer Warnes and Bill Medley
4 'Wind Beneath My Wings', Bette Midler
5 'Pie Jesu', Requiem
6 'Candle in the Wind', Elton John
7 'With or Without You', U2
8 'Tears in Heaven', Eric Clapton
9 'Every Breath You Take', The Police
10 'Unchained Melody', Righteous Brothers

Source: The Bereavement Register

HIGHEST-EARNING FILMS IN THE WORLD

	Film	Year	Total world gross
1	*Titanic**	1997	$1,845,034,188
2	*The Lord of the Rings: The Return of the King*	2003	$1,129,219,252
3	*Pirates of the Caribbean: Dead Man's Chest*	2006	$1,066,179,725
4	*Harry Potter and the Sorcerer's Stone*	2001	$985,817,659
5	*Pirates of the Caribbean: At World's End*	2007	$961,002,663
6	*Harry Potter and the Order of the Phoenix*	2007	$938,465,035
7	*The Lord of the Rings: The Two Towers*	2002	$926,287,400
8	*Star Wars: Episode I – The Phantom Menace*	1999	$924,317,554
9	*Shrek 2†*	2004	$920,665,658
10	*Jurassic Park*	1993	$914,691,118

* Won Best Picture Oscar
† Animated

MOST PROFITABLE FILMS OF ALL TIME

	Film/year	Budget	Total world gross *	Profit ratio
1	*The Blair Witch Project*, 1999	$35,000	$248,662,839	7,104.65
2	*Rocky†*, 1976	$1,100,000	$225,000,000	204.55
3	*American Graffiti*, 1973	$750,000	$115,000,000	153.33
4	*Snow White and the Seven Dwarfs‡*, 1937	$1,488,000	$187,670,866	126.12
5	*The Rocky Horror Picture Show*, 1975	$1,200,000	$139,876,417	116.56
6	*Gone With the Wind†*, 1939	$3,900,000	$390,525,192	100.13
7	*Saw*, 2004	$1,200,000	$103,096,345	85.91
8	*E.T. The Extra-Terrestrial*, 1982	$10,500,000	$792,910,554	75.52
9	*My Big Fat Greek Wedding*, 2002	$5,000,000	$368,744,044	73.75
10	*The Full Monty*, 1997	$3,500,000	$257,850,122	73.67

* Minimum entry $100 million world gross
† Won Best Picture Oscar
‡ Animated

BIGGEST FILM FLOPS OF ALL TIME

	Film/year	Budget	Total world gross*	Total receipts as % of budget
1	*Eye See You*, 2002	$55,000,000	$79,161	0.14
2	*The Adventures of Pluto Nash*, 2002	$100,000,000	$7,103,972	7.1
3	*Lolita*, 1997	$62,000,000	$5,173,783	8.34
4	*Moneybone*, 2001	$75,000,000	$7,622,365	10.16
5	*Town & Country*, 2001	$90,000,000	$10,372,291	11.52
6	*Cutthroat Island*, 1995	$98,000,000	$12,258,974	12.51
7	*Gigli*, 2003	$54,000,000	$7,266,209	13.46
8	*A Sound of Thunder*, 2005	$80,000,000	$11,665,465	14.58
9	*Dudley Do-Right*, 1999	$70,000,000	$10,316,055	14.73
10	*Stay*, 2005	$50,000,000	$8,342,132	16.68

* Films with estimated budgets of $50 million+

FILMS IN THE UK

	Film	Year	Total UK box office gross
1	*Titanic**	1998	**£69,025,646**
2	*Harry Potter and the Sorcerer's Stone*	2001	**£66,096,060**
3	*The Lord of the Rings: The Fellowship of the Ring*	2001	**£63,051,172**
4	*The Lord of the Rings: The Return of the King**	2003	**£61,062,348**
5	*The Lord of the Rings: The Two Towers*	2002	**£57,654,384**
6	*Casino Royale*	2006	**£55,502,884**
7	*Harry Potter and the Chamber of Secrets*	2002	**£54,780,731**
8	*The Full Monty*	1997	**£52,232,058**
9	*Pirates of the Caribbean: Dead Man's Chest*	2006	**£51,993,705**
10	*Star Wars: Episode I – The Phantom Menace*	1999	**£51,063,811**

* Won Best Picture Oscar

DIRECTORIAL DEBUT FILMS*

	Film	Year	Director	Total world gross
1	*American Beauty*	1999	Sam Mendes	$356,296,601
2	*Love Actually*	2003	Richard Curtis	$246,942,017
3	*American Pie*	1999	Paul Weitz†	$235,483,004
4	*Con Air*	1997	Simon West	$224,012,234
5	*Alien 3*	1992	David Fincher	$159,773,545
6	*Mousehunt*	1997	Gore Verbinski	$125,947,102
7	*Star Trek VII: Generations*	1994	David Carson	$119,971,125
8	*The Hitchhiker's Guide to the Galaxy*	2005	Garth Jennings	$104,478,416
9	*Mad Max*	1980	George Miller	$99,750,000
10	*Star Trek III: The Search for Spock*	1984	Leonard Nimoy	$87,071,046

* Full-length feature films
† With brother, Chris Weitz (uncredited)

FILM-PRODUCING COUNTRIES

	Country	Feature films produced, 2006
1	India	1,091
2	USA	490
3	Japan	417
4	China	330
5	France	203
6	Russia	200
7	Spain	150
8	Brazil	142
9	UK	134
10	Germany	122

Source: *Screen Digest*

Based on the number of full-length feature films produced, Hollywood's 'golden age' was the 1920s and 1930s, with 854 films made in 1921, and its nadir 1978, with just 354. Even the output of India's mighty film industry has dwindled slightly since its 2002 peak, when some 1,200 films were made.

COUNTRIES BY BOX-OFFICE REVENUE

	Country	Estimated total box-office gross, 2006
1	USA	$9,420,000,000
2	Japan	$1,839,600,000
3	UK	$1,397,000,000
4	France	$1,387,600,000
5	Germany	$1,018,300,000
6	Spain	$788,300,000
7	Canada	$685,900,000
8	Italy	$680,200,000
9	Australia	$661,000,000
10	Mexico	$557,900,000

Source: Screen Digest

BESTSELLING DVDS IN THE UK

1 *The Lord of the Rings: The Fellowship of the Ring*
2 *The Lord of The Rings: The Two Towers*
3 *The Lord of the Rings: The Return of the King*
4 *Pirates of the Caribbean: The Curse of the Black Pearl*
5 *Shrek 2*
6 *Harry Potter and the Prisoner of Azkaban*
7 *Finding Nemo*
8 *The Matrix*
9 *Harry Potter and the Chamber of Secrets*
10 *Love Actually*

Source: British Video Association/The Official UK Charts Company

TOP 10
MOST-RENTED DVDS IN THE UK *

1   *Four Weddings and a Funeral*
2   *Dirty Dancing*
3   *Basic Instinct*
4   *Crocodile Dundee*
5   *Gladiator*
6   *Sister Act*
7   *Forrest Gump*
8   *The Sixth Sense*
9   *Home Alone*
10 *Ghost*

* Includes VHS and DVD formats
Source: British Video Association/MRIB

FIRST *CARRY ON* FILMS

	Film	UK release
1	*Carry On Sergeant*	Aug 1958
2	*Carry On Nurse*	Feb 1959
3	*Carry On Teacher*	Aug 1959
4	*Carry On Constable*	Feb 1960
5	*Carry On Regardless*	Mar 1961
6	*Carry On Cruising*	Apr 1962
7	*Carry On Cabby*	Jun 1963
8	*Carry On Jack*	Nov 1963
9	*Carry On Spying*	Jun 1964
10	*Carry On Cleo*	Nov 1964

This original series of hugely successful British comedy films spanned 20 years. The first 10 were followed by *Carry On Cowboy*, *Carry On Screaming*, *Carry On – Don't Lose Your Head*, *Carry On – Follow That Camel*, *Carry On Doctor*, *Carry On Up the Khyber*, *Carry On Again Doctor*, *Carry On Camping*, *Carry On Up the Jungle*, *Carry On Loving*, *Carry On Henry*, *Carry On at Your Convenience*, *Carry On Abroad*, *Carry On Matron*, *Carry On Girls*, *Carry On Dick*, *Carry On Behind*, *Carry On England* and *Carry On Emmannuelle*, the last of the series released in 1978. *Carry on Columbus* (1992) was an attempt to revive the series.

COMEDY FILMS*

	Film	Year	Total world gross
1	*Pirates of the Caribbean: Dead Man's Chest*	2006	$1,066,179,725
2	*Pirates of the Caribbean: At World's End*	2007	$961,002,663
3	*Forrest Gump†*	1994	$677,387,716
4	*Pirates of the Caribbean: The Curse of the Black Pearl*	2003	$654,264,015
5	*Men in Black*	1997	$589,390,539
6	*Night at the Museum*	2006	$573,558,399
7	*Home Alone*	1990	$533,761,243
8	*Meet the Fockers*	2004	$516,642,939
9	*Ghost*	1990	$505,702,588
10	*Bruce Almighty*	2003	$484,572,835

* Live-action only, excluding animated
† Won Best Picture Oscar

HIGHEST-GROSSING HORROR FILMS

	Film	Year	Total world gross
1	*Jurassic Park*	1993	$914,691,118
2	*The Sixth Sense*	1999	$672,804,617
3	*The Lost World: Jurassic Park*	1997	$618,638,999
4	*I Am Legend*	2007	$510,982,867
5	*Jaws*	1975	$470,653,000
6	*The Mummy Returns*	2001	$433,013,274
7	*The Mummy*	1999	$415,933,406
8	*Signs*	2002	$408,247,917
9	*Godzilla*	1998	$379,014,294
10	*Jurassic Park III*	2001	$368,780,809

This list encompasses supernatural and science-fiction horror films featuring monster creatures such as dinosaurs and oversized sharks.

HORROR SPOOF FILMS

	Film	Year	Total world gross
1	*Scary Movie*	2000	**$278,019,771**
2	*Scary Movie 3*	2003	**$220,673,217**
3	*Scary Movie 4*	2006	**$178,262,620**
4	*Scream*	1996	**$172,967,847**
5	*Scream 2*	1997	**$172,363,301**
6	*Scream 3*	2000	**$161,834,276**
7	*Scary Movie 2*	2001	**$141,220,678**
8	*The Rocky Horror Picture Show*	1975	**$139,876,417**
9	*Young Frankenstein*	1974	**$86,273,333**
10	*Lake Placid*	1999	**$56,870,414**

While many films combine comedy and horror elements – among them *Ghoulies* (1985), the two *Gremlins* films (1984 and 1990), *Little Shop of Horrors* (1986) and *Arachnophobia* (1990) – those in this Top 10 represent the most successful of a species of parodies of classic horror films that began 60 years ago with such examples as *Abbott and Costello Meet Frankenstein* (1948).

JAMES BOND FILMS

	Film	Bond actor	Year	Total world gross
1	*Casino Royale*	Daniel Craig	2006	**$594,239,066**
2	*Die Another Day*	Pierce Brosnan	2002	**$456,042,139**
3	*The World is Not Enough*	Pierce Brosnan	1999	**$390,000,000**
4	*GoldenEye*	Pierce Brosnan	1995	**$352,194,034**
5	*Tomorrow Never Dies*	Pierce Brosnan	1997	**$339,340,102**
6	*Moonraker*	Roger Moore	1979	**$202,708,099**
7	*For Your Eyes Only*	Roger Moore	1981	**$195,300,000**
8	*The Living Daylights*	Timothy Dalton	1987	**$191,200,897**
9	*Octopussy*	Roger Moore	1983	**$187,493,619**
10	*The Spy Who Loved Me*	Roger Moore	1977	**$185,438,673**

Ian Fleming wrote 12 James Bond novels, only three of which, *Casino Royale*, *Moonraker* and *The Spy Who Loved Me*, figure in this Top 10. After his death in 1964, *For Your Eyes Only*, *Octopussy*, *The Living Daylights* and *GoldenEye* were developed by other writers from his short stories, while subsequent releases were written without reference to Fleming's work. The original film of *Casino Royale* (1967), featuring 56-year-old David Niven as the retired spy Sir James Bond, is an oddity in that it was presented as a comedy. This and *Never Say Never Again* (1983), effectively a remake of *Thunderball*, are not considered 'official' Bond films, making the 2006 *Casino Royale* the 21st in the canonical series.

FIRST BOND GIRLS

	Bond girl*	Actress	Film	Year
1	Honey Ryder	Ursula Andress	*Dr. No*	1962
2	Tatiana Romanova	Daniela Bianchi	*From Russia with Love*	1963
3	Pussy Galore	Honor Blackman	*Goldfinger*	1964
4	Domino Derval	Claudine Auger	*Thunderball*	1965
5	Kissy Suzuki	Mie Hama	*You Only Live Twice*	1967
6	Tracy Draco	Diana Rigg	*On Her Majesty's Secret Service*	1969
7	Tiffany Case	Jill St John	*Diamonds are Forever*	1971
8	Solitaire	Jane Seymour	*Live and Let Die*	1973
9	Mary Goodnight	Britt Ekland	*The Man with the Golden Gun*	1974
10	Major Anya Amasova	Barbara Bach	*The Spy Who Loved Me*	1977

* Principals only; minor roles omitted

Kim Basinger appeared as Domino in *Never Say Never Again* (1983), which is not included in the Bond franchise and is effectively a remake of *Thunderball*.

SUPERHERO FILMS

	Film	Year	Total world gross
1	*Spider-Man 3*	2007	$890,871,626
2	*Spider-Man*	2002	$821,708,551
3	*Spider-Man 2*	2004	$783,964,497
4	*The Incredibles**	2004	$631,442,092
5	*X-Men: The Last Stand*	2006	$459,256,008
6	*Batman*	1989	$413,388,924
7	*X2: X-Men United*	2003	$407,557,613
8	*Superman Returns*	2006	$391,081,192
9	*Batman Begins*	2005	$371,853,783
10	*The Mask*	1994	$351,583,407

* Animated

WAR FILMS

	Film/setting	Year	Total world gross
1	*Troy* (Trojan wars)	2004	**$497,409,852**
2	*Saving Private Ryan* (Second World War)	1998	**$481,803,460**
3	*The Last Samurai* (Japanese Emperor vs. samurai)	2003	**$456,758,981**
4	*300* (Battle of Thermopylae)	2007	**$456,068,181**
5	*Pearl Harbor* (Second World War)	2001	**$450,524,710**
6	*Gone With the Wind* (US Civil War)	1939	**$390,525,192**
7	*Schindler's List* (Second World War)	1993	**$321,307,716**
8	*The English Patient* (Second World War)	1996	**$233,816,374**
9	*Life is Beautiful* (*La Vita è bella*) (Second World War)	1997	**$229,358,132**
10	*Master and Commander: The Far Side of the World* (Napoleonic Wars)	2003	**$210,550,863**

* Won Best Picture Oscar

X-RATED FILMS OF ALL TIME

	Film	Year	Total world gross
1	*The Exorcist*	1973	$441,071,011
2	*Saturday Night Fever*	1978	$285,400,000
3	*The Godfather*	1972	$245,044,459
4	*One Flew Over the Cuckoo's Nest*	1975	$112,000,000
5	*Alien*	1979	$104,931,801
6	*The Godfather Part II*	1972	$102,600,000
7	*Mad Max*	1979	$99,750,000
8	*Amityville Horror*	1979	$86,432,520
9	*Apocalypse Now*	1979	$78,784,010
10	*10*	1979	$74,865,517

The British Board of Film Censors (now called the British Board of Film Classification) began issuing certificates in 1913. At that time, the distinction was between 'U' (universal) and 'A' (adult), although at first this was advisory only. The designation 'H' for horror films was added in 1933 and 'X' for 'adults only' from 9 January 1951. Further revisions took place in 1970 and again on 1 November 1982, when 'X' was replaced by '18' and 'A' by 'PG' (parental guidance), while 'U' has been retained. These are the highest earning films to be given an X-certificate in the UK in the period 1951–82. The classification of many films was subsequently altered – *Saturday Night Fever*, for example, was cut and re-released in 1979 as an 'A'.

ANIMATED FILMS

	Film	Year	Total world gross
1	*Shrek 2**	2004	**$920,665,658**
2	*Finding Nemo†*	2003	**$864,625,978**
3	*Shrek the Third**	2007	**$794,289,493**
4	*The Lion King†*	1994	**$783,841,776**
5	*Ice Age: The Meltdown‡*	2006	**$651,564,512**
6	*The Incredibles†*	2004	**$631,442,092**
7	*Ratatouille†*	2007	**$620,236,276**
8	*Madagascar**	2005	**$532,680,671**
9	*Monsters, Inc.†*	2001	**$529,061,238**
10	*The Simpsons Movie‡*	2007	**$526,551,795**

* DreamWorks
† Disney
‡ 20th Century Fox Animation

FILMS TO WIN THE MOST OSCARS

	Film	Year	Nominations	Awards
1=	*Ben-Hur*	1959	12	11
=	*Titanic*	1997	14	11
=	*The Lord of the Rings: The Return of the King*	2003	11	11
4	*West Side Story*	1961	11	10
5=	*Gigi*	1958	9	9
=	*The Last Emperor*	1987	9	9
=	*The English Patient*	1996	12	9
8=	*Gone With the Wind*	1939	13	8*
=	*From Here to Eternity*	1953	13	8
=	*On the Waterfront*	1954	12	8
=	*My Fair Lady*	1964	12	8
=	*Cabaret*†	1972	10	8
=	*Gandhi*	1982	11	8
=	*Amadeus*	1984	11	8

* Plus two special awards
† Did not win Best Picture Oscar

Ten other films have won seven Oscars each: *Going My Way* (1944), *The Best Years of Our Lives* (1946), *The Bridge on the River Kwai* (1957), *Lawrence of Arabia* (1962), *Patton* (1970), *The Sting* (1973), *Out of Africa* (1985), *Dances with Wolves* (1991), *Schindler's List* (1993) and *Shakespeare in Love* (1998). Like *Titanic* (1997), *All About Eve* (1950) received 14 nominations, but won in only six categories.

ACTORS AND ACTRESSES WITH THE MOST OSCAR NOMINATIONS*

	Actor	Wins Supporting	Best	Nominations
1	Meryl Streep	1	1	14
2=	Katharine Hepburn	0	4	12
=	Jack Nicholson	1	2	12
4=	Bette Davis	0	2	10
=	Laurence Olivier	0	1	10
6=	Paul Newman	0	1	9
=	Spencer Tracy	0	2	9
8=	Marlon Brando	0	2	8
=	Jack Lemmon	1	1	8
=	Peter O'Toole	0	0	8
=	Al Pacino	0	1	8
=	Geraldine Page	0	1	8

* In all acting categories

As well as his nine acting nominations, Paul Newman received one as a director and has won an Honorary Oscar and the prestigious Jean Hersholt Humanitarian Award.

BRITISH ACTORS AND ACTRESSES WITH THE MOST OSCAR NOMINATIONS*

	Actor	Wins Supporting	Best	Nominations
1	Laurence Olivier	0	1	10
2	Peter O'Toole	0	0	8
3=	Richard Burton	0	0	7
=	Greer Garson	0	1	7
5=	Michael Caine	2	0	6
=	Judi Dench	1	0	6
=	Deborah Kerr	0	0	6
=	Vanessa Redgrave	1	0	6
=	Maggie Smith	1	1	6
10=	Olivia de Havilland†	0	2	5
=	Albert Finney	0	0	5
=	Kate Winslet	0	0	5

* In all acting categories
† British-born, naturalized US citizen 1941

LATEST WINNERS OF *ADULT VIDEO NEWS* BEST PERFORMERS OF THE YEAR

	Female	Male
2008	Sasha Grey	Evan Stone
2007	Hillary Scott	Tommy Gunn
2006	Audrey Hollander	Manuel Ferrara
2005	Lauren Phoenix	Manuel Ferrara
2004	Ashley Blue	Michael Stefano
2003	Aurora Snow	Lexington Steele
2002	Nikita Denise	Lexington Steele
2001	Jewel De'Nyle	Evan Stone
2000	Inari Vachs	Lexington Steele
1999	Chloe	Tom Byron

First presented in 1986, the American *Adult Video News* awards acknowledge performers as well as creators and distributors of pornographic films.

THE 10 LATEST GOLDEN RASPBERRIES 'WORST' AWARDS

	Worst film	Worst actress	Worst actor
2007	*I Know Who Killed Me*	Lindsay Lohan	Eddie Murphy
2006	*Basic Instinct 2*	Sharon Stone	Marlon and Shawn Waynans
2005	*Dirty Love*	Jenny McCarthy	Rob Schneider
2004	*Catwoman*	Halle Berry	George W. Bush*
2003	*Gigli*	Jennifer Lopez	Ben Affleck
2002	*Swept Away*	Madonna	Roberto Benigni
2001	*Freddy Got Fingered*	Mariah Carey	Tom Green
2000	*Battlefield Earth*	Madonna	John Travolta
1999	*Wild Wild West*	Heather Donahue	Adam Sandler
1998	*An Alan Smithee Film: Burn Hollywood Burn*	The Spice Girls	Bruce Willis

* For his 'starring' role in *Fahrenheit 9/11*
Source: Golden Raspberry Awards

LONGEST-RUNNING PROGRAMMES ON BBC RADIO

	Programme	First broadcast
1	*Radio 4 Appeal**	24 Jan 1926
2	*The Shipping Forecast*	26 Jan 1926
3	*Choral Evensong*	7 Oct 1926
4	*Daily Service*	2 Jan 1928†
5	*The Week in Westminster*	6 Nov 1929
6	*Sunday Half Hour*	14 Jul 1940
7	*Desert Island Discs*	29 Jan 1942
8	*Composer of the Week‡*	2 Aug 1943
9	*From Our Own Correspondent*	4 Oct 1946
10	*Woman's Hour*	7 Oct 1946

* Formerly *The Week's Good Cause*
† Experimental broadcast; national transmission began December 1929
‡ Formerly *This Week's Composer*

The BBC's London station 2LO had first broadcast a programme called *Woman's Hour* on 2 May 1923, but the current series began in 1946. Other programmes from the 1940s that are still aired include *Round Britain Quiz* (2 November 1947 – formerly *Transatlantic Quiz*, which started on 29 July 1945), *Any Questions?* (12 October 1948) and *Book at Bedtime* (6 August 1949). *Gardeners' Question Time* was first broadcast on 9 April 1947 as *How Does Your Garden Grow?* Its name was changed in 1950. A pilot for *The Archers* was broadcast in the Midland region for a one-week trial beginning on 29 May 1950, but the serial did not begin its national run until 1 January 1951.

TELEVISION-WATCHING COUNTRIES*

	Country	Average daily viewing time per household Hours	Minutes
1	USA	8	11
2	Turkey	5	0
3	Italy	4	6
4	Belgium†	3	50
5	Japan	3	43
6	Spain	3	37
7	Portugal	3	32
8	Australia	3	12
9	South Korea	3	10
10	Canada	3	5
	UK	*3*	*0*

* OECD countries, 2005 or latest available year
† Walloon-speaking
Source: OECD, *Communications Outlook 2007*

TELEVISION AUDIENCES IN THE UK

	Programme	Broadcast	Audience
1	1966 World Cup Final: England vs. West Germany	30 Jul 1966	**32,300,000**
2	Funeral of Princess Diana	6 Sep 1997	**32,100,000**
3	*The Royal Family* documentary	21 Jun 1969	**30,690,000**
4	*EastEnders* (Den divorces Angie)	25 Dec 1986	**30,150,000**
5	Apollo 13 splashdown	17 Apr 1970	**28,600,000**
6	Cup Final Replay: Chelsea vs. Leeds United	28 Apr 1970	**28,490,000**
7	Wedding of Prince Charles and Lady Diana Spencer	29 Jul 1981	**28,400,000**
8	Wedding of Princess Anne and Captain Mark Phillips	14 Nov 1973	**27,600,000**
9	*Coronation Street* (Alan Bradley killed)	19 Mar 1989	**26,930,000**
10	*Only Fools and Horses* (Batman and Robin episode)	29 Dec 1996	**24,350,000**

Source: British Film Institute

LONGEST-RUNNING PROGRAMMES ON BRITISH TELEVISION

	Programme	First broadcast
1	*Panorama*	11 Nov 1953
2	*What the Papers Say*	5 Nov 1956
3	*The Sky at Night*	24 Apr 1957
4	*Blue Peter*	16 Oct 1958
5	*Coronation Street*	9 Dec 1960
6	*Songs of Praise*	1 Oct 1961
7	*Horizon*	2 May 1964
8	*Match of the Day*	22 Aug 1964
9	*The Money Programme*	5 Apr 1966
10	*A Question of Sport*	5 Jan 1970

COUNTRIES WITH HIGHEST PROPORTION OF FEMALE WORKERS

	Country	Labour force percentage*
1	Mozambique	53.5
2	Burundi	51.9
3	Cambodia	51.4
4	Rwanda	51.2
5	Malawi	49.8
6	Kazakhstan	49.6
7=	Estonia	49.4
=	Tanzania	49.4
9	Belarus	49.3
10=	Armenia	49.2
=	Lithuania	49.2
	World average	*40.1*
	USA	*46.2*
	UK	*46*

* Aged 15–64 who are currently employed; unpaid groups are not included
Source: World Bank, *World Development Indicators 2007*

TOP 10

COUNTRIES WITH LOWEST PROPORTION OF FEMALE WORKERS

	Country	Labour force percentage*
1	United Arab Emirates	13.4
2	Saudi Arabia	15.2
3	Oman	16.4
4	Egypt	21.7
5	Jordan	24.4
6	Sudan	24.8
7	Kuwait	25.4
8	Morocco	25.5
9	Turkey	26.4
10	Pakistan	27

* Aged 15–64 who are currently employed; unpaid groups are not included
Source: World Bank, *World Development Indicators 2007*

Although not an independent country, the Palestinian territories of West Bank and Gaza have a female employment rate of just 13.1 per cent.

MOST STRESSFUL JOBS IN THE UK*

1   Prison officer
2   Police
3   Social work
4   Teaching
5   Ambulance service
6   Nursing
7   Medicine
8   Fire fighting
9   Dentistry
10 Mining

* Based on assessments of the stress levels of 104 jobs by Professor Cary Cooper at the University of Manchester's Institute of Science and Technology

LEAST STRESSFUL JOBS IN THE UK*

1 Librarian
2 Museum personnel
3 Biologist
4 Nursery nurse
5 Astronomer
6 Beauty therapist
7 Linguist
8 Remedial gymnast
9 Speech therapist
10 Chemist

* Based on assessments of the stress levels of 104 jobs by Professor Cary Cooper at the University of Manchester's Institute of Science and Technology

OLDEST-ESTABLISHED BUSINESSES IN THE UK

	Business/location	Founded
1	Kirkstall Forge (ironworks), Kirkstall, Leeds	1200
2	The Shore Porters Society of Aberdeen, Aberdeen	1498
3	Cambridge University Press (publishers), Cambridge	1534
4	John Brooke and Sons (property management), Huddersfield	1541
5	Child's Bank (now part of Royal Bank of Scotland) London	1559
6	Whitechapel Bell Foundry, London	1570
7	Oxford University Press (publishers), Oxford	1585
8	Richard Durtnell and Sons (builders), Brasted, nr Westerham, Kent	1591
9	Tissimans & Sons Ltd (clothing), Bishop's Stortford	1601
10	Hays at Guildford (office services), Guildford (formerly London)	1651

The companies listed, and certain others, belong to an elite group of tercentenarians, firms that have been in business for 300 years or more. A few have even been under the control of the same family for their entire history. Although not a 'business', by some criteria the Royal Mint (founded in 886 in London, now relocated to Cardiff) may claim to predate all these enterprises.

RETAILERS IN THE UK

	Store group	Annual sales*
1	Tesco	£39,454,000,000
2	J. Sainsbury	£16,061,000,000
3	W. M. Morrison	£12,461,500,000
4	Kingfisher (B&Q, etc.)	£8,675,900,000
5	Marks & Spencer	£7,797,700,000
6	DSG (Dixons)	£7,403,400,000
7	John Lewis Partnership	£6,400,000,000
8	Home Retail (Argos, Homebase)	£5,851,000,000
9	Boots	£5,027,400,000
10	Inchcape (automotive)	£4,842,100,000

* To year ending 31 December 2006 or closest accounting period

MOBILE PHONE-USING COUNTRIES

	Country	Mobile subscribers
1	China	461,058,000
2	USA	233,000,000
3	India	166,050,000
4	Russia	150,000,000
5	Japan	101,698,000
6	Brazil	99,918,600
7	Germany	84,300,000
8	Italy	78,571,000
9	UK	69,656,600
10	France	51,662,000
	World total	*2,719,604,400*

THE 10

MOST DANGEROUS JOBS IN THE UK*

1   Bomb disposal officer
2   Deep-sea diver
3   Deep-sea fisherman
4   Demolition worker
5   Fast-jet pilot
6   Oil platform worker
7   Professional motor/motorcycle racer
8   Professional stuntman
9   Steeplejack
10   Tunneller (face worker)

* In alphabetical order

Life assurance companies base their premiums on actuarial statistics that take into account the likelihood of people in each job being involved in an accident that injures or kills them at work, or as a result of their contact with dangerous substances. This does not mean that assurance companies will not provide cover for such professions, but the riskier the job, the higher the premium. According to one well-known life assurance company, the most risky job is that of a mercenary – but they qualify this by indicating that they would not actually insure someone claiming this profession.

THE 10
WORST INDUSTRIAL DISASTERS*

Location/date/incident	Number killed
1 Bhopal, India, 3 Dec 1984 Methylisocyante gas escape at Union Carbide plant	**3,849**
2 Jesse, Nigeria, 17 Oct 1998 Oil pipeline explosion	**>700**
3 Oppau, Germany, 21 Sep 1921 Bradishe Aniline chemical plant explosion	**561**
4 San Juanico, Mexico, 19 Nov 1984 Explosion at a PEMEX liquified petroleum gas plant	**540**
5 Cubatão, Brazil, 25 Feb 1984 Oil pipeline explosion	**508**
6 Durunkah, Egypt, 2 Nov 1994 Fuel storage depot fire	**500**
7 Mexico City, Mexico, 19 Nov 1984 Butane storage explosion	**400**
8 Adeje, Nigeria, 10 Jul 2000 Oil pipeline explosion	**250**
9 Guadalajara, Mexico, 22 Apr 1992 Explosions caused by a gas leak into sewers	**230**
10 Oakdale, Pennsylvania, 18 May 1918 TNT explosion at Aetna Chemical Company	**210**

* Including industrial sites, factories, fuel depots and pipelines; excluding military, munitions, bombs, mining, marine and other transport disasters, dam failures and mass poisonings

THE 10
WORST EXPLOSIONS*

	Location/date/incident	Estimated number killed
1	**Rhodes, Greece, 3 Apr 1856** Lightning strike of gunpowder store	**4,000**
2	**Breschia, Italy, 18 Aug 1769** Church of San Nazaire caught fire after being struck by lightning and gunpowder store exploded	**3,000**
3=	**Salang Tunnel, Afghanistan, 3 Nov 1982** Petrol tanker collision	**2,000**
=	**Lanchow, China, 26 Oct 1935** Arsenal	**2,000**
5	**Halifax, Nova Scotia, 6 Dec 1917** Ammunition ship *Mont Blanc*	**1,963**
6	**Hamont Station, Belgium, 3 Aug 1918** Ammunition trains	**1,750**
7	**Memphis, USA, 27 Apr 1865** Paddlesteamer *Sultana* boiler explosion	**1,547**
8=	**Archangel, Russia, 20 Feb 1917** Munitions ship	**1,500**
=	**Smederovo, Yugoslavia, 9 Jun 1941** Ammunition dump	**1,500**
10	**Bombay, India, 14 Apr 1944** Ammunition ship *Fort Stikine*	**1,376**

* Excluding mining disasters, terrorist and military bombs and natural explosions, such as volcanoes

MOST VALUABLE TRADED METALLIC ELEMENTS*

	Element	Price ($ per kg)
1	Rhodium	$227,622
2	Platinum	$53,562
3	Gold	$29,489
4	Iridium	$14,306
5	Ruthenium	$12,860
6	Osmium	$12,217
7	Palladium	$12,168
8	Rhenium	$9,700
9	Germanium	$1,275
10	Gallium	$600

* Based on 10–100 kg quantities of minimum 99.9% purity; excluding radioactive elements, isotopes and rare earth elements traded in minute quantities, as at 28 January 2008
Source: Lipmann Walton, *London Metal Bulletin*, W. C. Heraeus GmbH & Co. KG and www.thebulliondesk.com

The prices of traded metals varies enormously according to their rarity, changes in industrial uses, fashion and popularity as investments. Since the start of the 21st century, the price of market-leader Rhodium has increased over eightfold and that of platinum more than quadrupled.

RICHEST COUNTRIES

	Country	Gross Domestic Product per capita, 2006
1	Luxembourg	$87,955
2	Norway	$72,306
3	Qatar	$62,914
4	Iceland	$54,858
5	Switzerland	$51,771
6	Denmark	$50,965
7	Ireland	$44,500
8	USA	$44,190
9	Sweden	$42,383
10	Netherlands	$40,571
	UK	*$39,213*

Source: International Monetary Fund

GDP (Gross Domestic Product) is the total value of all the goods and services produced annually within a country (Gross National Product, GNP, also includes income from overseas). Dividing GDP by the country's population produces GDP per capita, which is often used as a measure of how 'rich' a country is. Some 51 industrialized nations have GDPs per capita in excess of $10,000, while about 24 developing countries, particularly those in Africa, have per capita GDPs of less than $500.

GOLD-PRODUCING COUNTRIES

	Country	Percentage of world total production	Production, 2006 (tonnes)
1	South Africa	11.8	291.8
2	USA	10.2	251.8
3	China	10	247.2
4	Australia	9.9	244.5
5	Peru	8.2	203.3
6	Russia	7	172.8
7	Indonesia	4.6	114.1
8	Canada	4.2	104
9	Uzbekistan	3.2	78.5
10	Ghana	2.8	70.2
	World total	*100*	*2,471.1*

Source: Gold Fields Mineral Services Ltd, *Gold Survey 2007*

COUNTRIES WITH THE MOST GOLD

	Country	Gold reserves* (tonnes)
1	USA	8,133.5
2	Germany	3,417.5
3	France	2,622.3
4	Italy	2,451.8
5	Switzerland	1,166.3
6	Japan	765.2
7	Netherlands	624.5
8	China	600
9	Russia	438.2
10	Taiwan	423.3
	UK	*310.3*
	World total	*29,955*

* As at December 2007
Source: World Gold Council

Gold reserves are the government holdings of gold in each country – which are often far greater than the gold owned by private individuals. In the days of the 'Gold Standard', this provided a tangible measure of a country's wealth, guaranteeing the convertibility of its currency, and determined such factors as exchange rates. Though less significant today, gold reserves remain a component in calculating a country's international reserves, alongside its holdings of foreign exchange and SDRs (Special Drawing Rights). In addition to the countries listed, the International Monetary Fund has 3,217.3 tonnes and the European Central Bank 604.7 tonnes. About a fifth of all the gold ever mined is in the world's gold reserves. If it were all made into a cube, it sides would measure 11.6 m (38 ft), fractionally wider than a tennis court.

MOST VALUABLE GLOBAL BRANDS

	Brand name*	Industry	Brand value, 2007
1	Coca-Cola	Beverages	$65,324,000,000
2	Microsoft	Technology	$58,709,000,000
3	IBM	Technology	$57,091,000,000
4	General Electric	Diversified	$51,569,000,000
5	Nokia, Finland	Technology	$33,696,000,000
6	Toyota, Japan	Automotive	$32,070,000,000
7	Intel	Technology	$30,954,000,000
8	McDonald's	Food retail	$29,398,000,000
9	Disney	Leisure	$29,210,000,000
10	Mercedes-Benz	Automotive	$23,568,000,000

* All US-owned unless otherwise stated
Source: Interbrand/*BusinessWeek*

Brand consultants Interbrand use a method of estimating value that takes account of the profitability of individual brands within a business (rather than the companies that own them), as well as such factors as their potential for growth.

RICHEST MEN*

	Name/country (citizen/ residence, if different)	Source	Net worth
1	William H. Gates III, USA	Microsoft (software)	$56,000,000,000
2	Warren Edward Buffett, USA	Berkshire Hathaway (investments)	$52,000,000,000
3	Carlos Slim Helu, Mexico	Communications	$49,000,000,000
4	Ingvar Kamprad, Sweden/ Switzerland	Ikea (home furnishings)	$33,000,000,000
5	Lakshmi Mittal, India/UK	Mittal Steel	$32,000,000,000
6	Sheldon Adelson, USA	Casinos and hotels	$26,500,000,000
7	Bernard Arnault, France	Louis Vuitton, etc. (luxury goods)	$26,000,000,000
8	Amancio Ortega, Spain	Zara, etc. (clothing)	$24,000,000,000
9	Li Ka-shing, China	Investments	$23,000,000,000
10	David Thomson, Canada	Media, entertainment	$22,000,000,000

* Excluding rulers and family fortunes
Source: *Forbes* magazine, 'The World's Billionaires', 2007

HIGHEST-EARNING CELEBRITIES

	Celebrity*	Profession	Earnings†
1	Oprah Winfrey	Talk show host/producer	$260,000,000
2	Jerry Bruckheimer	Film and TV producer	$120,000,000
3	Steven Spielberg	Film producer/director	$110,000,000
4	Tiger Woods	Golfer	$100,000,000
5	Johnny Depp	Film actor	$92,000,000
6	Jay-Z	Hip-Hop impresario	$83,000,000
7	Tom Hanks	Film actor	$74,000,000
8	Madonna	Singer	$72,000,000
9	Howard Stern	Radio shock jock	$70,000,000
10	Bon Jovi	Singer	$67,000,000

* Individuals, excluding groups; all US
† 2006–7
Source: *Forbes* magazine, 'The Celebrity 100', 2007

HIGHEST-EARNING DEAD CELEBRITIES

	Celebrity	Profession	Death	Earnings 2006–7
1	Elvis Presley	Rock star	16 Aug 1977	**$49,000,000**
2	John Lennon	Rock star	8 Dec 1980	**$44,000,000**
3	Charles Schultz	'Peanuts' cartoonist	12 Feb 2000	**$35,000,000**
4	George Harrison	Rock star	29 Nov 2001	**$22,000,000**
5	Albert Einstein	Scientist	18 Apr 1955	**$18,000,000**
6	Andy Warhol	Artist	22 Feb 1987	**$15,000,000**
7	Theodor 'Dr Seuss' Geisel	Author	24 Sep 1991	**$13,000,000**
8	Tupac Shakur	Musician	13 Sep 1996	**$9,000,000**
9	Marilyn Monroe	Actress	5 Aug 1962	**$7,000,000**
10	Steve McQueen	Actor	30 Nov 1980	**$6,000,000**

Source: *Forbes magazine*, 'Top-Earning Dead Celebrities', 2007

RICHEST BRITISH-BORN PEOPLE

	Name	Source	Net worth
1	The Duke of Westminster	Property	£7,000,000,000
2	Philip and Tina Green	Retailing	£4,900,000,000
3	Jim Ratcliffe	Chemicals	£3,300,000,000
4	Sir Richard Branson	Transport and mobile phones	£3,100,000,000
5	Sean Quinn	Cement, etc.	£3,050,000,000
6	Joseph Lewis	Finance	£2,800,000,000
7	Earl Cadogan and family	Property	£2,610,000,000
8	Bernie Ecclestone	Motor racing	£2,250,000,000
9	Lord Sainsbury and family	Supermarkets	£2,130,000,000
10=	Richard Desmond	Publishing	£1,900,000,000
=	Roddie Fleming and family	Finance	£1,900,000,000
=	Eddie and Malcolm Healey	Property and kitchens	£1,900,000,000

Source: *Sunday Times* Rich List, 2007

LARGEST YACHTS

	Yacht	Owner	Built/refitted	Length
1	*Al Salamah*	King Fahd, Saudi Arabia	1999	**139.8 m** (456 ft 10 in)
2	*Rising Sun*	Larry Ellison, USA	2004	**138.4 m** (452 ft 8 in)
3	*Octopus*	Paul Allen, USA	2003	**126.1 m** (414 ft)
4	*Savarona*	Kahraman Sadikoglu, Turkey (charter)	1931/ 1992	**124.3 m** (408 ft)
5	*Alexander*	Latsis family, Greece	1976/ 1986	**122 m** (400 ft 2 in)
6	*Turama*	Latsis family, Greece	1990/ 2004	**116.9 m** (381 ft 9 in)
7	*Atlantis II*	Niarchos family, Greece	1981	**115.6 m** (379 ft 7 in)
8	*Pelorus*	Roman Abramovich, Russia	2003	**114.9 m** (377 ft 3 in)
9	*Le Grand Bleu*	Roman Abramovich	2000	**112.7 m** (370 ft)
10	*Lady Moura*	Nasser al-Rashid, Saudi Arabia	1990	**104.8 m** (344 ft)

Source: *Power & Motoryacht*, 2007

HOTTEST CHILLIES

	Chilli*	Scoville units
1	Naga Jolokia	855,000–1,041,427
2	Red Savina	350,000–577,000
3	Datil, Habanero, Scotch Bonnet	100,000–350,000
4	African Birdseye, Jamaican Hot, Rocoto	100,000–200,000
5	Chiltepin, Malaqueta, Pequin, Santaka, Thai	50,000–100,000
6	Ají, Cayenne, Tabasco	30,000–50,000
7	de Arbol	15,000–30,000
8	Serrano, Yellow Wax	5,000–15,000
9	Chipotle, Jalapeño, Mirasol	2,500–5,000
10	Cascabel, Rocotillo, Sandia, Sriracha	1,500–2,500

* Typical examples – there are others in most categories

Hot peppers contain substances called capsaicinoids, which determine how 'hot' they are. In 1912 American pharmacist Wilbur Lincoln Scoville (1865–1942) pioneered a test, based on which chillies are ranked by Scoville units. According to this scale, one part of capsaicin, the principal capsaicinoid, per million equals 15,000 Scoville units. Pure capsaicin registers 15,000,000–17,000,000 on the Scoville scale – one drop diluted with 100,000 drops of water will still blister the tongue – while at the other end of the scale bell peppers and pimento register zero.

TOP 10

SMELLIEST FRENCH CHEESES

1 Vieux Boulogne
   Cow's milk cheese from Boulogne-sur-Mer, 7–9 weeks old

2 Pont l'Evêque AOC*
   Cow's milk cheese from Normandy, 6 weeks old

3 Camembert de Normandie AOC
   Cow's milk cheese from Normandy, minimum 21 days old

4 Munster
   Cow's milk cheese from Alsace Lorraine, 3 weeks old

5 Brie de Meaux AOC
   Cow's milk cheese from Ile de France, 4–8 weeks old

6 Roquefort AOC
   Sheep's milk cheese from Roquefort, 3 months old

7 Reblochon AOC
   Cow's milk cheese from Savoie, 3–4 weeks old

8 Livarot AOC
   Cow's milk cheese from Normandy, 90 days old

9 Banon AOC
   Goat's milk cheese from Provence, 1–2 weeks old

10 Epoisses de Bourgogne AOC
   Cow's milk cheese from Burgundy, 4–6 weeks old

* AOC = Appellation d'Origine Contrôlée – there are 41 such French cheeses

'Smelliest' tends to be down to a personal assessment, but a recent survey at Cranfield University on which this list is based employed 19 expert members of a human olfactory panel and a high-tech 'electronic nose'. Although 10th on the list, Epoisses de Bourgogne is banned on public transport in France.

BEAN* CONSUMERS

	Country	Estimated consumption per capita, 2007
1	UK	5.78 kg (12 lb 12 oz)
2	Ireland	4.18 kg (9 lb 3 oz)
3	Portugal	3.13 kg (6 lb 14 oz)
4	Australia	2.25 kg (4 lb 15 oz)
5	Spain	2.1 kg (4 lb 10 oz)
6	Canada	2.09 kg (4 lb 10 oz)
7	USA	1.79 kg (3 lb 15 oz)
8	New Zealand	1.68 kg (3 lb 11 oz)
9	Saudi Arabia	1.66 kg (3 lb 11 oz)
10	France	1.49 kg (3 lb 5 oz)
	World average	*0.29 kg (10 oz)*

* Including baked beans, flageolet beans, kidney beans, chickpeas, lentils, broad beans, white beans, black beans, etc.; excludes beans canned with sausages, which are categorized as 'canned ready meals'
Source: Euromonitor International, Global Market Information Database

The world eats 1,890,610 tonnes of beans a year, of which the UK consumes 350,810 tonnes, or 18.6 per cent. Heinz baked beans are the best-known brand. They were originally test-marketed in the north of England in 1901 and imported from the USA up to 1928, when they were first canned here. The slogan 'Beanz Meanz Heinz' was invented in 1967 over a drink in the Victoria pub in Mornington Terrace by Young and Rubicam advertising agency executive Maurice Drake. Some 1.2 million cans of Heinz baked beans are eaten every day in the UK – worth £175,222,000 in 2006.

MEAT* CONSUMERS

	Country	Average consumption per capita, 2007
1	Spain	113.85 kg (251 lb)
2	Argentina	113.02 kg (249 lb 3 oz)
3	Australia	106.07 kg (233 lb 14 oz)
4	New Zealand	103.18 kg (227 lb 8 oz)
5	Austria	102.55 kg (226 lb 1 oz)
6	Portugal	102.32 kg (225 lb 9 oz)
7	Greece	101.66 kg (224 lb 2 oz)
8	USA	93.51 kg (206 lb 2 oz)
9	Ireland	83.8 kg (184 lb 12 oz)
10	France	83.67 kg (184 lb 7 oz)
	UK	*50.87 kg (112 lb 2 oz)*
	World average	*36.74 kg (81 lb)*

* Includes beef, veal, lamb, mutton, goat, pork, poultry and other meat
Source: Euromonitor International, Global Market Information Database

The world devours a total of 240,702,850 tonnes of meat a year.

ONE MAN'S MEAT

FOODS CONSUMED IN THE UK

	Item	Average weekly consumption per head*
1	Milk and cream	2,027 g (71.5 oz)
2	Soft drinks	1,718 g (60.6 oz)
3	Fresh fruit	1,292 g (45.57 oz)
4	Vegetables (excluding potatoes)	1,156 g (40.77 oz)
5	Meat and meat products	1,047 g (36.99 oz)
6	Cereals†	925 g (32.62 oz)
7	Fresh and processed potatoes	842 g (28.7 oz)
8	Alcoholic drinks	739 g (26.06 oz)
9	Bread	701 g (24.72 oz)
10	Fats	183 g (6.45 oz)

* Household purchases (excluding eating out) 2005–6
† Excluding bread
Source: Department for Environment, Food and Rural Affairs (Defra), 'Family Food 2005–6', 2007

TOP 10
PIZZAEXPRESS PIZZAS

1 Margherita (mozzarella and tomato)

2 American (pepperoni sausage)

3 Pollo ad Astra (torn chicken breast, peppadew sweet peppers, Cajun sauce, garlic and onions)

4 American Hot (pepperoni sausage, tomato and hot green peppers)

5 La Reine (prosciutto cotto ham, olives and mushrooms)

6 Sloppy Giuseppe (hot spiced beef, green peppers and onions)

7 Padana (goat's cheese, spinach, red onion and caramelized onion confit)

8 Etna (hot soft Calabrian salami, sweet roquito peppers, smoky speck ham, grana padano cheese and jalapenos on a Romana base)

9 Fiorentina (spinach, grana padano, egg, garlic and olives)

10 Giardiniera (asparagus, artichokes, mushrooms, red peppers, Santos tomatoes, olives and garlic on tomato and pesto sauce)

PizzaExpress founder Peter Boizot opened Britain's first Italian-style pizza restaurant in Wardour Street, London, in 1965. Among his innovations were the introduction of live jazz and the Pizza Veneziana, from which a percentage of every sale goes to the Venice in Peril Fund, with more than £1.6 million being raised so far. The chain now numbers 340 across the country. These are its Top 10 most popular types of pizza, with the recently launched Romana bases proving especially popular with men.

FAST-FOOD CHAINS IN THE UK (BY MARKET SHARE)

	Chain	% of total market
1	McDonald's	30
2	Yum! Brands (KFC, Taco Bell, Pizza Hut, etc.)	12.4
3	Burger King	12.3
4	Greggs (Baker's Oven, etc.)	11.1
5	Doctor's Associates (Subway)	8.6
6	Pret a Manger	2.6
7	Wimpy	1.9
8=	Cooks Ltd	1.8
=	Southern Fried Chicken	1.8
10	British Petroleum	1.5

Source: Euromonitor International

CONFECTIONERY BRANDS IN THE UK

	Brand/manufacturer	Sales, 2006*
1	Cadbury's Dairy Milk	£361,500,000
2	Wrigley's Extra	£169,400,000
3	Galaxy	£159,200,000
4	KitKat	£140,500,000
5	Maltesers	£121,000,000
6	Mars	£102,100,000
7	Quality Street	£73,100,000
8	Bassetts Allsorts, etc.	£72,700,000
9	Haribo gum	£71,700,000
10	Twix	£71,200,000

* Tracked through a total of 74,042 multiple and independent outlets
Source: *Checkout*, A. C. Nielsen

ALCOHOL-CONSUMING COUNTRIES

	Country	Consumption per capita (pure alcohol equivalent)
1	Luxembourg	12.6 litres (22.2 pints)
2	Hungary	11.4 litres (20.1 pints)
3	Czech Republic	11 litres (19.4 pints)
4	Ireland	10.8 litres (19 pints)
5	Germany	10.2 litres (17.9 pints)
6	Spain	10 litres (17.6 pints)
7=	Portugal	9.6 litres (16.9 pints)
=	UK	9.6 litres (16.9 pints)
9	Denmark	9.5 litres (16.7 pints)
10	Austria	9.3 litres (16.4 pints)
	USA	*6.8 litres (12 pints)*

DRINK BRANDS IN THE UK

	Brand	Type	Estimated sales range, 2007
1	Stella Artois	Lager	£320–325,000,000
2	Carling	Lager	£170–175,000,000
3	Hardys	Wine	£160–165,000,000
4	Fosters	Lager	£140–145,000,000
5	Ernest & Julio Gallo	Wine	£135–145,000,000
6	Carlsberg	Lager	£120–125,000,000
7	Blossom Hill	Wine	£110–115,000,000
8	Smirnoff Red Label	Vodka	£95–100,000,000
9	Carlsberg Export	Lager	£90–95,000,000
10=	Baileys	Whiskey and cream liqueur	£80–85,000,000
=	Budweiser	Lager	£80–85,000,000
=	The Famous Grouse	Whisky	£80–85,000,000
=	Grolsch	Lager	£80–85,000,000

Source: TNS Wordpanel

BEER-DRINKING COUNTRIES

	Country	Annual consumption per capita
1	Czech Republic	156.9 litres (276.1 pints)
2	Ireland	131.1 litres (230.7 pints)
3	Germany	115.8 litres (203.8 pints)
4	Australia	109.9 litres (193.4 pints)
5	Austria	108.3 litres (190.6 pints)
6	UK	99 litres (174.2 pints)
7	Belgium	93 litres (163.7 pints)
8	Denmark	89.9 litres (158.2 pints)
9	Finland	85 litres (149.6 pints)
10	Luxembourg	84.4 litres (148.5 pints)
	USA	*81.6 litres (143.6 pints)*

Source: Kirin

BEER BRANDS IN THE UK

	Brand	Estimated sales range, 2007
1	Stella Artois	£320–325,000,000
2	Carling	£170–175,000,000
3	Fosters	£140–145,000,000
4	Carlsberg	£120–125,000,000
5	Carlsberg Export	£90–95,000,000
6	Budweiser	£80–85,000,000
7	Grolsch	£80–85,000,000
8	Kronenbourg 1664	£70–75,000,000
9	Carlsberg Special Brew	£50–55,000,000
10	John Smith's Extra Smooth	£45–50,000,000

Source: TNS Worldpanel

WINE-DRINKING COUNTRIES

	Country	Consumption per capita, 2005
1	Vatican City	62.02 litres (35.24 pints)
2	Andorra	60.13 litres (34.17 pints)
3	France	55.85 litres (31.74 pints)
4	Luxembourg	52.7 litres (29.95 pints)
5	Italy	48.16 litres (27.37 pints)
6	Portugal	46.67 litres (26.52 pints)
7	Slovenia	43.77 litres (24.87 pints)
8	Croatia	42.27 litres (24.02 pints)
9	Switzerland	39.87 litres (22.66 pints)
10	Spain	34.66 litres (19.7 pints)
	UK	*18.97 litres (10.78 pints)*

Source: Wine Institute

MOST COMMON PUB NAMES IN THE UK

1   The Red Lion
2   The Crown
3   The Royal Oak
4   The White Hart
5   The King's Head
6   The Bull
7   The Coach and Horses
8   The George/George and Dragon
9   The Plough
10 The Swan

It is estimated that there are 58,197 pubs in the UK: 51,479 in England and Wales, 5,150 in Scotland and 1,568 in Northern Ireland. Among them there are perhaps more than 25,000 different names, of which the Red Lion, with over 600, is the most common. It probably derives from the lion featured on the coat of arms of John of Gaunt, Duke of Lancaster. Although there is little dispute about the frontrunners in this list, the continual renaming of pubs by breweries (in one case, for example, changing them all to the Rat and Carrot) is playing havoc with identifying the runners-up, even by the country's leading experts, and it would be fair to mention that the Bell, Rose and Crown, New Inn, White Horse and Anchor may arguably claim places in the Top 10.

LATEST PUBS OF THE YEAR

2007	The Old Spot Inn, Dursley, Gloucestershire
2006	Tom Cobley Tavern, Spreyton, Devon
2005	The Swan, Little Totham, Essex
2004	The Fat Cat, Norwich
2003	Crown & Thistle, Gravesend, Kent
2002	The Swan, Little Totham, Essex
2001	The Nursery, Heaton Norris, Greater Manchester
2000	Blisland Inn, Blisland, Cornwall
1999	The Rising Sun, Tipton, West Midlands
1998	The Fat Cat, Norwich

Source: CAMRA

MOST POPULAR COCKTAILS AT THE SAVOY HOTEL'S AMERICAN BAR

1   Dry Martini (gin and vermouth)

2   Whisky Sour (whisky and fresh lemon juice)

3   Tom Collins (gin, lemon juice, Gomme syrup and soda water)

4   Ricky (gin, lime, Gomme syrup and soda water)

5   Bloody Mary (vodka, tomato juice and spices)

6   White Lady (gin, lemon juice and Cointreau)

7   Sidecar (brandy, Cointreau and lemon juice)

8   Screwdriver (vodka and orange juice)

9   Old Fashioned (sugar cube, Angostura bitters, rye whisky, brandy, gin or rum)

10 Manhattan (rye whisky or bourbon, sweet vermouth and a dash of Angostura bitters)

The Savoy Hotel in London opened in 1889. It is closed for major renovation and scheduled to reopen in 2009. Its 'American Bar' (so called because it served ice in drinks – once regarded as a shocking American innovation) became world famous for its cocktails. Its barman Harry Craddock compiled *The Savoy Cocktail Book* (1930). Cocktails date from America in the early 19th century, but were drunk in London by the 1850s and became particularly fashionable in the 1920s. The origin of the word 'cocktail' has been the subject of much debate, and many far-fetched explanations have been proposed: it appears to have been first used in New Orleans and, as the city had strong French connections, some authorities trace it to the French *coquetier*, an eggcup – perhaps used as a measure for the ingredients – while others prefer to see a link to the 'cock-ale' once fed to fighting cocks.

LATEST HOLDERS OF THE LAND SPEED RECORD

	Driver/car	Date	Speed
1	Andy Green (UK), *ThrustSSC**	15 Oct 1997	1,227.99 km/h (763.04 mph)
2	Richard Noble (UK), *Thrust2**	4 Oct 1983	1,013.47 km/h (633.47 mph)
3	Gary Gabelich (USA), *The Blue Flame*	23 Oct 1970	995.85 km/h (622.41 mph)
4	Craig Breedlove (USA), *Spirit of America – Sonic 1*	15 Nov 1965	960.96 km/h (600.6 mph)
5	Art Arfons (USA), *Green Monster*	7 Nov 1965	922.48 km/h (576.55 mph)
6	Craig Breedlove (USA), *Spirit of America – Sonic 1*	2 Nov 1965	888.76 km/h (555.48 mph)
7	Art Arfons (USA), *Green Monster*	27 Oct 1964	858.73 km/h (536.71 mph)
8	Craig Breedlove (USA), *Spirit of America*	15 Oct 1964	842.04 km/h (526.28 mph)
9	Craig Breedlove (USA), *Spirit of America*	13 Oct 1964	749.95 km/h (468.72 mph)
10	Art Arfons (USA), *Green Monster*	5 Oct 1964	694.43 km/h (434.02 mph)

* Location, Black Rock Desert, Nevada, USA; all other speeds were achieved at Bonneville Salt Flats, Utah, USA

FASTEST PRODUCTION CARS

	Car	Year	Bhp	Speed
1	SSC Ultimate Aero TT	2007	1,183	411.76 km/h (256.18 mph)
2	Bugatti Veyron	2004	1,001	408.47 km/h (253.81 mph)
3	Saleen S7	2005	750	402 km/h (250 mph)
4	Koenigsegg CCX	2006	806	395 km/h (245 mph)
5	McLaren F1	1994	620	386.4 km/h (240.1 mph)
6	Lamborghini Murciélago LP640	2006	640	352 km/h (219 mph)
7=	Ferrari Enzo	2002	657	349.2 km/h (217 mph)
=	Jaguar XJ220	1992	549	349.2 km/h (217 mph)
9	Bugatti EB110	1992	542	347.6 km/h (216 mph)
10	Ascari A10	2006	625	346 km/h (215 mph)

It has been claimed that it is technically impossible to build a road car capable of more than 402 km/h (250 mph), but the first two of these supercars have tipped over that theoretical limit. The list includes the fastest example of each marque, but excludes 'limited edition' cars and 'specials', such as the 410-km/h (255-mph) Porche GT9 by 9ff.

MOST EXPENSIVE CAR REGISTRATION NUMBERS SOLD AT AUCTION IN THE UK

	Number	Year	Price*
1	F1	2008	£440,625
2	M1	2006	£331,500
3	VIP 1†	2006	£285,000
4	GS 1	2005	£258,775
5	51 NGH	2006	£254,000
6	K1 NGS	1993	£235,000
7	1 OO	2006	£197,000
8	1A	1989	£176,000
9	CEO 1‡	2007	£154,000
10	1F	2005	£144,000

* Prices include buyer's premium
† Bought by Roman Abramovich
‡ The highest-priced registration number sold on eBay

LATEST CAR OF THE YEAR WINNERS

	Make/model
2008	Fiat Nuova 500
2007	Ford S-Max
2006	Renault Clio
2005	Toyota Prius
2004	Fiat Panda
2003	Renault Mégane
2002	Peugeot 307
2001	Alfa Romeo 147
2000	Toyota Yaris
1999	Ford Focus

The Car of the Year is an award made each November by leading motoring journalists, who vote for the best new car to go on sale across Europe in the preceding 12 months. The award was first presented in 1964, when it was won by the Rover 2000.

FASTEST PRODUCTION MOTORCYCLES

	Make/model	Speed
1	Suzuki GSX1300R Hayabusa	309 km/h (192 mph)
2	Kawasaki Ninja ZX-14	299 km/h (186 mph)
3=	Honda CBR1100XX Blackbird	291 km/h (181 mph)
=	Honda RC45(m)	291 km/h (181 mph)
5=	Harris Yamaha YZR500	289 km/h (180 mph)
=	Kawasaki ZZR1100 D7	289 km/h (180 mph)
7	Bimota YB10 Biposto	283 km/h (176 mph)
8	Suzuki GSX-R1100WP(d)	280 km/h (174 mph)
9	Suzuki GSX-R750-WV	279 km/h (173 mph)*
10=	Bimota Furano	278 km/h (173 mph)
=	Kawasaki ZZR1100 C1	278 km/h (173 mph)

* Top speed 173.5 mph

MOTOR VEHICLE-OWNING COUNTRIES

	Country	Cars	Commercial vehicles	Total (2005)
1	USA	132,908,828	104,788,269	237,697,097
2	Japan	57,090,789	16,733,871	73,824,660
3	Germany	46,090,303	3,133,197	49,223,500
4	Italy	34,667,485	4,422,269	39,089,754
5	France	29,990,000	6,139,000	36,039,000
6	UK	30,651,700	3,942,700	34,594,400
7	Russia	25,285,000	5,705,000	30,990,000
8	China	8,900,000	21,750,000	30,650,000
9	Spain	20,250,377	4,907,867	25,158,244
10	Brazil	18,370,000	4,653,000	23,023,000
	World total	617,020,169	245,108,745	862,128,914

Source: *Ward's Motor Vehicle Facts & Figures 2007*

CAR MANUFACTURERS

	Company/country	Passenger car production, 2006
1	Toyota (Japan)	6,800,228
2	General Motors (USA)	5,708,038
3	Volkswagen group (Germany)	5,429,896
4	Ford (USA)	3,800,633
5	Honda (Japan)	3,549,787
6	PSA Peugeot Citroën (France)	2,961,437
7	Nissan (Japan)	2,512,519
8	Hyundai (South Korea)	2,231,313
9	Renault-Dacia-Samsung (France)	2,085,837
10	Suzuki (Japan)	2,004,310
	World total (including manufacturers outside Top 10)	*51,953,234*

Source: OICA Statistics Committee

BESTSELLING CARS OF ALL TIME

	Manufacturer/model	Years in production	Approximate sales*
1	Toyota Corolla	1966–	31,600,000
2	Volkswagen Golf	1974–	24,000,000
3	Volkswagen Beetle	1937–2003†	21,529,464
4	Ford Escort/Orion	1968–2003	20,000,000
5	Ford Model T	1908–27	16,536,075
6	Honda Civic	1972–	16,500,000
7	Nissan Sunny/ Sentra/Pulsar	1966–	16,000,000
8	Volkswagen Passat	1973–‡	15,000,000
9	Lada Riva	1980–	13,500,000
10	Chevrolet Impala/ Caprice	1958–	13,000,000

* To 2006, except where otherwise indicated
† Produced in Mexico 1978–2003
‡ Still manufactured in Ukraine and Egypt

Estimates of manufacturers' output of their bestselling models vary from the approximate to the unusually precise 16,536,075 of the Model T Ford, with 15,007,033 produced in the USA and the rest in Canada and the UK, between 1908 and 1927. It should be noted that while some of the models listed remained distinctive throughout their lifespan, others appear under the same name but with different stylings around the world and have undergone such major design overhauls (at least nine in the case of the list-leading Toyota Corolla) that, while they remain members of the same family, the current cars may be considered distant relatives of the vehicles with which the model was launched.

CAR-PRODUCING COUNTRIES

	Country	Car production, 2006
1	Japan	9,756,515
2	Germany	5,398,508
3	China	5,233,132
4	USA	4,366,220
5	South Korea	3,489,136
6	France	2,723,196
7	Brazil	2,092,029
8	Spain	2,078,639
9	India	1,473,000
10	UK	1,442,085

Source: OICA Statistics Committee

THE 10

WORST AIR DISASTERS IN THE WORLD

Location/date/incident	Number killed

1 New York, USA, 11 Sep 2001 — *c.* **1,622**

Following a hijacking by terrorists, an American Airlines Boeing 767 was deliberately flown into the North Tower of the World Trade Center, killing all 81 passengers (including five hijackers), 11 crew on board and an estimated 1,530 on the ground, both as a direct result of the crash and in the subsequent fire and collapse of the building, which also killed 479 rescue workers.

2 New York, USA, 11 Sep 2001 — *c.* **677**

As part of the coordinated attack, hijackers commandeered a second Boeing 767 and crashed it into the South Tower of the World Trade Center, killing all 56 passengers and nine crew on board and approximately 612 on the ground.

3 Tenerife, Canary Islands, 27 Mar 1977 — **583**

Two Boeing 747s (Pan-Am and KLM, carrying 380 passengers and 16 crew and 234 passengers and 14 crew respectively) collided and caught fire on the runway of Los Rodeos airport after the pilots received incorrect control-tower instructions. A total of 61 escaped.

4 Mt Ogura, Japan, 12 Aug 1985 — **520**

A JAL Boeing 747 on an internal flight from Tokyo to Osaka crashed, killing all but four of the 509 passengers and all 15 crew on board.

5 Charkhi Dadri, India, 12 Nov 1996 — **349**

Soon after taking off from New Delhi's India Gandhi International Airport, a Saudi Arabian Airlines Boeing 747 collided with a Kazakh Airlines Ilyushin IL-76 cargo aircraft on its descent and exploded, killing all 312 (289 passengers and 23 crew) on the Boeing and all 37 (27 passengers and 10 crew) on the Ilyushin in the world's worst mid-air crash.

6 Paris, France, 3 Mar 1974 — **346**

Immediately after take-off for London, a Turkish Airlines DC-10 suffered an explosive decompression when a door burst open and crashed at Ermenonville, north of Paris, killing all 335 passengers, including many England rugby supporters, and its crew of 11.

7   Off the Irish coast, 23 Jun 1985   **329**
     An Air India Boeing 747 on a flight from Vancouver to Delhi exploded in mid-air,
     probably as a result of a terrorist bomb, killing all 307 passengers and 22 crew.

8   Riyadh, Saudi Arabia, 19 Aug 1980   **301**
     Following an emergency landing a Saudia (Saudi Arabian) Airlines Lockheed
     TriStar caught fire. The crew were unable to open the doors and all 287
     passengers and 14 crew died from smoke inhalation.

9   Off the Iranian coast, 3 Jul 1988   **290**
     An Iran Air A300 airbus was shot down in error by a missile fired by the USS
     Vincennes, which mistook the airliner for an Iranian fighter aircraft, resulting in
     the deaths of all 274 passengers and 16 crew. In 1996 the US paid $61.8 million
     in compensation to the families of the victims.

10   Sirach Mountain, Iran, 19 Feb 2003   **275**
     An Ilyushin 76 on a flight from Zahedan to Kerman crashed into the mountain in
     poor weather. It was carrying 257 Revolutionary Guards and a crew of 18, none
     of whom survived.

The UK's worst disaster was Pan Am Flight 103 from London Heathrow to New York,
which exploded in mid-air as a result of a terrorist bomb and crashed onto Lockerbie,
Scotland, on 21 December 1988, killing a total of 270 (243 passengers, 16 crew and 11
on the ground) in the UK's worst-ever air disaster. The worst prior to that was the crash
of British European Airways Trident at Staines, Middlesex, on 18 June 1972, which left
118 dead.

In addition to disasters within the UK, a number of major air crashes involving British
aircraft have occurred overseas, among them that of a BOAC Boeing 707 that crashed
on Mount Fuji, Japan, on 5 March 1966, killing 124 (the day after a crash near by killed
64), and in the crash of a Dan Air Boeing 727 at Santa Cruz de Tenerife, Canary Islands,
on 25 April 1980 (all 146 on board perished). The collision of a British Airways Trident
heading from London to Istanbul and an Inex Adria DC-9 over Zagreb on 10 September
1976 left 176 dead, 54 passengers and nine crew in the British aircraft and 108
passengers and five crew in the Yugoslavian aircraft.

LONGEST MOTORWAYS IN THE UK

	Motorway	Route	Length
1	M6	Rugby–Carlisle	364.8 km (226.7 miles)
2	M1	London–Leeds	307.1 km (190.8 miles)
3	M4	London–Pont Abraham	305 km (189.5 miles)
4	M5	Birmingham–Exeter	262.2 km (162.9 miles)
5	M25	Circles London	188.3 km (117 miles)
6	M62	Liverpool–Humberside	173.3 km (107.7 miles)
7	M40	Birmingham–London	143.2 km (89 miles)
8=	M3	London–Southampton	94.3 km (58.6 miles)
=	M11	London–Cambridge	80 km (49.7 miles)
10	M8	Edinburgh–Glasgow Airport	78.4 km (48.7 miles)

Britain's first motorway was the Preston bypass section of the M6 (between junctions 29 and 32), opened on 5 December 1958. The first section of the M1 did not open until 2 November 1959.

BUSIEST LONDON UNDERGROUND STATIONS

	Station	Annual number of passengers, 2006*
1	Victoria	72,992,000
2	Waterloo	72,874,000
3	Oxford Circus	68,438,000
4	Liverpool Street	57,895,000
5	King's Cross St Pancras	52,510,000
6	Paddington	38,718,000
7	Bank and Monument	38,209,000
8	Piccadilly Circus	37,633,000
9	Tottenham Court Road	32,843,000
10	Bond Street	32,760,000

*Estimated total number of passengers using the station in both directions

A total of over 1.3 billion journeys a year are made on the London Underground (a third of them via the Top 10 stations), with a weekday average of 3.4 million passengers a day. The annual total number of passengers using Victoria, the busiest tube station, is more than the entire population of the UK.

TOP 10

MOST COMMON TYPES OF PROPERTY LOST ON LONDON TRANSPORT

	Type	Number of items found 2005–2006
1	Cases and bags	26,247
2	Books, chequebooks and credit cards	25,146
3	Clothing	22,484
4	'Value items' (handbags, purses, wallets, etc.)	14,937
5	Mobile telephones	13,767
6	Keys	8,123
7	Umbrellas	6,839
8	Spectacles	6,633
9	Jewellery, cameras, laptop computers, etc.	5,684
10	Gloves (pairs; single =497)	3,088

Source: Transport for London Lost Property Office

Books (along with chequebooks and credit cards, which are included with them) have dropped from their long-standing No. 1 position. Changes in fashion mean that hats, once one of the most common lost items, no longer even warrant a separate category, whereas mobile telephones are now lost in increasing numbers. Of the total, some 30 per cent of lost property is restored to its owners, but as much as 55 per cent of valuable items are returned. Among the stranger items that have been lost in recent years are a skeleton, a box of glass eyes, breast implants, artificial legs and hands, a Yamaha outboard motor, a complete double bed, a theatrical coffin, a wedding dress, a stuffed gorilla and an urn containing human ashes.

TOURIST DESTINATIONS

	Country	International visitors, 2006
1	France	79,100,000
2	Spain	58,500,000
3	USA	51,100,000
4	China	49,600,000
5	Italy	41,100,000
6	UK	30,700,000
7	Germany	23,600,000
8	Mexico	21,400,000
9	Austria	20,300,000
10	Russia	20,200,000
	World total	*846,000,000*

Source: World Tourism Organization

FASTEST ROLLER-COASTERS

	Roller-coaster/location	Year opened	Speed
1	Kingda Ka, Six Flags Great Adventure, Jackson, New Jersey, USA	2005	**206 km/h (128 mph)**
2	Top Thrill Dragster, Cedar Point, Sandusky, Ohio, USA	2003	**193 km/h (120 mph)**
3	Dodonpa, Fuji-Q Highlands, Fujiyoshida, Yamanashi, Japan	2001	**172 km/h (107 mph)**
4=	Superman the Escape, Six Flags Magic Mountain, Valencia, California, USA	1997	**161 km/h (100 mph)**
=	Tower of Terror, Dreamworld, Coomera, Queensland, Australia	1997	**161 km/h (100 mph)**
6	Steel Dragon 2000, Nagashima Spa Land, Nagashima, Mie, Japan	2006	**153 km/h (95 mph)**
7	Millennium Force, Cedar Point, Sandusky, Ohio, USA	2000	**150 km/h 93 mph)**
8=	Goliath, Six Flags Magic Mountain, Valencia, California, USA	2000	**137 km/h (85 mph)**
=	Titan, Six Flags Over Texas, Arlington, Texas, USA	2001	**137 km/h (85 mph)**
10	Furius Baco, Port Aventura, Salou, Tarragona, Spain	2007	**135 km/h (84 mph)**

TOURIST DESTINATIONS OF UK RESIDENTS

	Country	Visitors, 2006
1	Spain	14,428,000
2	France	10,854,000
3	Ireland	4,682,000
4	USA	3,986,000
5	Italy	3,380,000
6	Germany	2,698,000
7	Greece	2,436,000
8	Netherlands	2,410,000
9	Portugal	1,937,000
10	Belgium	1,815,000
	Total (all countries)	*69,536,000*

Source: National Statistics, *Travel Trends 2006*

TOP 10

TOURIST ATTRACTIONS IN THE UK*

	Attraction/location	Visitors, 2006
1	Blackpool Pleasure Beach	5,730,000
2	British Airways London Eye	3,500,000
3	Tower of London	2,084,468
4	Kew Gardens, London	1,357,522
5	Edinburgh Castle	1,213,907
6	Chester Zoo	1,161,922
7	The Eden Project, Cornwall	1,152,332
8	Canterbury Cathedral	1,047,380
9	Westminster Abbey, London	1,028,991
10	Roman Baths and Pump Room, Bath	986,720

* Excluding museums and art galleries
Source: Association of Leading Visitor Attractions (ALVA) and British Airways/London Eye

GOALSCORERS IN THE FIFA WORLD CUP*

	Player/country	Years	Goals
1	Ronaldo, Brazil	1998–2006	15
2	Gerd Müller, West Germany	1970–74	14
3	Just Fontaine, France	1958	13
4	Pelé, Brazil	1958–70	12
5=	Sándor Kocsis, Hungary	1954	11
=	Jürgen Klinsman, Germany	1990–98	11
7=	Helmut Rahn, West Germany	1954–8	10
=	Teófilio Cubillas, Peru	1970–78	10
=	Grzegorz Lato, Poland	1974–82	10
=	Gary Lineker, England	1986–90	10
=	Gabriel Batistuta, Argentina	1994–2002	10
=	Miroslav Klose, Germany	2002–6	10

* In the final stages, 1930–2006
† Fontaine's total of 13 goals in 1958 is a record for one tournament

TOP 10

BRITISH FOOTBALL TEAMS IN EUROPE*

Team	CL W	CL RU	UE W	UE RU	FA W	FA RU	CWC W	CWC RU	SC W	SC RU	Total points
1 Liverpool	5	1	3	0	0	1	3	2	11	4	26
2= Arsenal	0	1	1	1	1	2	0	1	2	5	9
= Manchester United	2	0	0	0	1	0	1	1	4	1	9
4= Leeds United	0	1	2	1	0	1	0	0	2	3	7
= Nottingham Forest	2	0	0	0	0	0	1	1	3	1	7
= Tottenham Hotspur	0	0	2	1	1	0	0	0	3	1	7
7 Chelsea	0	0	0	0	2	0	1	0	3	0	6
8 Glasgow Rangers	0	0	0	0	1	2	0	1	1	3	5
9= Aberdeen	0	0	0	0	1	0	1	0	2	0	4
= Aston Villa	1	0	0	0	0	0	1	0	2	0	4
= Celtic	1	1	0	1	0	0	0	0	1	2	4

* All competitions up to and including 2006–7 season, based on two points for winning the four main competitions and one point for being runner-up. The four main competitions are the Champions League (CL; formerly the Champions' Cup), the UEFA Cup (UEFA; formerly the Fairs Cup), the Cup-winners' Cup (CWC) and Super Cup (SC)

The first British team to win a European competition was Tottenham Hotspur in 1963, when they beat Atletico Madrid 5–1 in Rotterdam to win the Cup-winners' Cup.

TOP 10

FA PREMIERSHIP GOALSCORERS*

	Players	Club(s)	Goals
1	Alan Shearer	Blackburn Rovers, Newcastle United	261
2	Andy Cole	Newcastle United, Manchester United, Blackburn Rovers, Fulham, Manchester City, Portsmouth, Birmingham City, Sunderland	187
3	Thierry Henry	Arsenal	174
4	Robbie Fowler	Liverpool, Leeds United, Manchester City	161
5	Les Ferdinand	Queens Park Rangers, Newcastle United, Tottenham Hotspur, West Ham United, Leicester City, Bolton Wanderers	150
6	Teddy Sheringham	Nottingham Forest, Tottenham Hotspur, Manchester United, Portsmouth, West Ham United	147
7	Jimmy Floyd Hasselbaink	Leeds United, Chelsea, Middlesbrough, Charlton Athletic	128
8	Michael Owen	Liverpool, Newcastle United	126
9	Dwight Yorke	Aston Villa, Manchester United, Blackburn Rovers, Birmingham, City, Sunderland	122
10	Ian Wright	Arsenal, West Ham United	113

* As at 1 January 2008

MOST POINTS IN A BARCLAYS PREMIER LEAGUE SEASON*

	Team	Season	Points
1	Chelsea	2004–5	95
2	Manchester United	1993–4	92
3=	Manchester United	1999–2000	91
=	Chelsea	2005–6	91
5	Arsenal	2003–4	90
6=	Blackburn Rovers	1994–5	89
=	Manchester United	2006–7	89
8	Manchester United†	1994–5	88
9	Arsenal	2001–2	87
10=	Manchester United	1992–3	84
=	Blackburn Rovers†	1993–4	84

* Up to and including 2006–7
† Team did not win the League title in season indicated

BARCLAYS PREMIER LEAGUE GOALSCORERS IN ONE SEASON*

	Player/club	Season	Goals
1=	Andy Cole, Newcastle United	1993–4	34
=	Alan Shearer, Blackburn Rovers	1994–5	34
3=	Alan Shearer, Blackburn Rovers	1993–4	31
=	Alan Shearer, Blackburn Rovers	1995–6	31
5=	Kevin Phillips, Sunderland	1999–2000	30
=	Thierry Henry, Arsenal	2003–4	30
7	Robbie Fowler, Liverpool	1995–6	28
8	Thierry Henry, Arsenal	2005–6	27
9=	Chris Sutton, Norwich City	1993–4	25
=	Matt Le Tissier, Southampton	1993–4	25
=	Robbie Fowler, Liverpool	1994–5	25
=	Les Ferdinand, Newcastle United	1995–6	25
=	Alan Shearer, Newcastle United	1996–7	25
=	Ruud Van Nistelrooy, Manchester United	2002–3	25
=	Thierry Henry, Arsenal	2004–5	25

* Premier League matches only, up to and including 2006–7

The first-ever Premier League goal was scored by Brian Deane of Sheffield United against Manchester United on the opening day of the 1992–3 season.

CLUBS WITH THE MOST BRITISH TITLES *

	Team	League titles	FA Cup	League Cup	Total
1	Glasgow Rangers	51	31	24	**106**
2	Glasgow Celtic	41	34	13	**88**
3	Liverpool	18	7	7	**32**
4	Manchester United	16	11	2	**29**
5	Arsenal	13	10	2	**25**
6	Aston Villa	7	7	5	**19**
7	Aberdeen	4	7	5	**16**
8	Heart of Midlothian	4	7	4	**15**
9	Everton	9	5	–	**14**
10	Tottenham Hotspur	2	8	3	**13**

* As at end of 2006–7 season

GOALSCORERS FOR UK INTERNATIONAL TEAMS

	Player/country	Years	Goals*
1	Bobby Charlton, England	1958–70	49
2	Gary Lineker, England	1984–92	48
3	Jimmy Greaves, England	1959–67	44
4	Michael Owen, England	1997–2006	36
5=	Tom Finney, England	1946–58	30
=	Nat Lofthouse, England	1950–58	30
=	Denis Law, Scotland	1959–74	30
=	Kenny Dalglish, Scotland	1972–87	30
=	Alan Shearer, England	1992–2000	30
10	Vivian Woodward, England	1903–11	29
	Ian Rush, Wales	*1980–96*	*28*
	David Healy, Northern Ireland	*2000–2008*	*33*

* As at 1 January 2007

THE 10
LATEST FOOTBALLERS
OF THE YEAR*

	Player/country	Club
2007	Cristiano Ronaldo, Portugal	Manchester United
2006	Thierry Henry, France	Arsenal
2005	Frank Lampard, England	Chelsea
2004	Thierry Henry, France	Arsenal
2003	Thierry Henry, France	Arsenal
2002	Robert Pires, France	Arsenal
2001	Teddy Sheringham, England	Manchester United
2000	Roy Keane, Ireland	Manchester United
1999	David Ginola, France	Tottenham Hotspur
1998	Dennis Bergkamp, Netherlands	Arsenal

* As voted by the Football Writers' Association (FWA)

The first winner of the FWA award was Stanley Matthews in 1948. The trophy presented to the winner is now called the Sir Stanley Matthews Trophy in his honour.

MEDAL-WINNING COUNTRIES AT THE SUMMER OLYMPICS

	Country	Gold	Silver	Bronze	Total
1	USA	907	697	615	**2,219**
2	USSR/Unified Team/Russia	525	436	409	**1,370**
3	Germany/West Germany	229	258	298	**785**
4	UK	189	242	237	**668**
5	France	199	202	230	**631**
6	Italy	189	154	168	**511**
7	Sweden	140	157	179	**476**
8	Hungary	158	141	161	**460**
9	East Germany	159	150	136	**445**
10	Australia	119	126	154	**399**

MEDAL-WINNING COUNTRIES AT THE WINTER OLYMPICS*

	Country	Gold	Silver	Bronze	Total†
1	Russia/USSR/Unified Team	122	89	86	**297**
2	Norway	96	102	84	**282**
3	USA	78	81	59	**218**
4	Germany/West Germany	76	78	57	**211**
5	Austria	50	64	71	**185**
6	Finland	42	57	52	**151**
7	Sweden	46	32	44	**122**
8	Canada	38	38	44	**120**
9	Switzerland	37	37	43	**117**
10	East Germany	39	37	35	**111**

* Up to and including the 2006 Turin Games
† Includes medals won at figure skating and ice hockey, which were part of the Summer Olympics prior to the inauguration of the Winter Games in 1924

THE 10

LATEST WINNERS OF THE BBC SPORTS PERSONALITY OF THE YEAR AWARD

	Winner	Sport
2007	Joe Calzaghe	Boxing
2006	Zara Phillips	Eventing
2005	Andrew Flintoff	Cricket
2004	Kelly Holmes	Athletics
2003	Jonny Wilkinson	Rugby Union
2002	Paula Radcliffe	Athletics
2001	David Beckham	Football
2000	Steve Redgrave	Rowing
1999	Lennox Lewis	Boxing
1998	Michael Owen	Football

Source: BBC

HIGHEST-EARNING BRITISH SPORTSMEN

	Sportsman	Sport	Estimated earnings, 2007
1	Michael Owen	Football	£37,000,000
2=	Jenson Button	Motor racing	£30,000,000
=	Wayne Rooney	Football	£30,000,000
4	David Beckham	Football	£16,500,000
5	Frank Lampard	Football	£15,000,000
6	Steven Gerrard	Football	£14,000,000
7=	Damien Duff	Football	£12,000,000
=	Emile Heskey	Football	£12,000,000
=	Harry Kewell	Football	£12,000,000
=	John Terry	Football	£12,000,000
=	Mike Welch	Football	£12,000,000

HIGHEST-EARNING WORLD SPORTSPEOPLE

	Sportsman/country*	Sport	Estimated earnings, 2006–7
1	Tiger Wood	Golf	$100,000,000
2	Oscar de la Hoya	Boxing	$43,000,000
3	Phil Mickelson	Golf	$42,200,000
4	Kimi Räikkönen, Finland	Motor racing	$40,000,000
5	Michael Schumacher, Germany	Motor racing	$36,000,000
6	David Beckham, UK	Football	$33,000,000
7	Kobe Bryant	Basketball	$32,900,000
8	Shaquille O'Neal	Basketball	$31,900,000
9=	Michael Jordan	Basketball	$31,000,000
=	Ronaldinho, Brazil	Football	$31,000,000

* All from the USA unless otherwise stated
Source: *Forbes* magazine

TOP 10

LARGEST SPORTS STADIUMS*

	Stadium	Location	Year opened	Capacity
1	Rungnado May Day Stadium	Pyöngyang, North Korea	1989	**150,000**
2	Saltlake Stadium	Calcutta, India	1984	**120,000**
3	Estádio Azteca	Mexico City, Mexico	1966	**114,465**
4	Michigan Stadium	Ann Arbor, Michigan, USA	1927	**107,501**
5	Beaver Stadium	Pennsylvania State University, USA	1960	**107,282**
6	Neyland Stadium	Knoxville, Tennessee, USA	1921	**104,079**
7	Ohio Stadium	Colombus, USA	1922	**101,568**
8	National Stadium	Kuala Lumpur, Malaysia Bukit Jalil	1998	**100,200**
9=	Azadi Stadium	Tehran, Iran	1971	**100,000**
=	Bung Karno Nehru Stadium	New Delhi, India	1982	**100,000**
=	Melbourne Cricket Ground	Melbourne, Australia	1853	**100,000**

* Based on official capacity 2007; excludes motor-racing and horse-racing tracks

MOST SUPERBOWL WINS*

Team	Appearances	Wins
1= Dallas Cowboys	1972, 1978, 1993–4, 1996	5
= Pittsburgh Steelers	1975–6, 1979–80, 2006	5
= San Francisco 49ers	1982, 1985, 1989–90, 1995	5
4= Green Bay Packers	1967–8, 1997	3
= Oakland/Los Angeles Raiders	1977, 1981, 1984	3
= Washington Redskins	1983, 1988, 1992	3
= New England Patriots	2002, 2004–5, 2008	3
= New York Giants	1987, 1991, 2008	3
9= Baltimore/ Indianapolis Colts	1971, 2007	2
= Miami Dolphins	1973–4	2
= Denver Broncos	1998–9	2

* Based on wins, up to and including Superbowl XLII (2008)

MOST WORLD SERIES WINS*

	Team	First	Wins Last	Total
1	New York Yankees	1923	2000	26
2	St. Louis Cardinals	1926	2006	10
3	Oakland Athletics (5 titles as Philadelphia Athletics)	1910	1989	9
4	Boston Red Sox	1903	2007	7
5	Los Angeles Dodgers (1 title as Brooklyn Dodgers)	1955	1988	6
6=	San Francisco Giants (all titles as New York Giants)	1905	1954	5
=	Pittsburgh Pirates	1909	1979	5
=	Cincinatti Reds	1919	1990	5
9	Detroit Tigers	1935	1984	4
10=	Chicago White Sox	1906	2005	3
=	Atlanta Braves (1 title as Boston Braves, 1 as Milwaukee Braves)	1914	1995	3
=	Minnesota Twins (1 title as Washington Senators)	1924	1991	3
=	Baltimore Orioles	1966	1983	3

* Up to and including 2007 World Series

MOST POINTS IN A SINGLE NBA GAME*

	Player/team	Opponents	Date	Points
1	Wilt Chamberlain, Philadelphia Warriors	New York Knicks	2 Mar 1962	**100**
2	Kobe Bryant, Los Angeles Lakers	Toronto Raptors	22 Jan 2006	**81**
3	Wilt Chamberlain, Philadelphia Warriors	Los Angeles Lakers	8 Dec 1961†	**78**
4=	Wilt Chamberlain, Philadelphia Warriors	Chicago Packers	13 Jan 1962	**73**
=	Wilt Chamberlain, San Francisco Warriors	New York Knicks	16 Nov 1962	**73**
=	David Thompson, Denver Nuggets	Detroit Pistons	9 Apr 1978	**73**
7	Wilt Chamberlain, San Francisco Warriors	Los Angeles Lakers	3 Nov 1962	**72**
8=	Elgin Baylor, Los Angeles Lakers	New York Knicks	15 Nov 1960	**71**
=	David Robinson, San Antonio Spurs	Los Angeles Clippers	24 Apr 1994	**71**
10	Wilt Chamberlain, San Francisco Warriors	Syracuse Nationals	10 Mar 1963	**70**

* As at the end of the 2006–7 season
† Including three periods of overtime

MOST WICKETS IN TEST CRICKET*

	Bowler/country	Years	Matches	Wickets
1	Muttiah Muralitharan, Sri Lanka	1992–2007	118	**723**
2	Shane Warne, Australia	1992–2007	145	**708**
3	Anil Kumble, India	1990–2008	118	**566**
4	Glenn McGrath, Australia	1993–2007	124	**563**
5	Courtney Walsh, West Indies	1984–2001	132	**519**
6	Kapil Dev, India	1978–94	131	**434**
7	Richard Hadlee, New Zealand	1973–90	86	**431**
8	Shaun Pollock, South Africa	1995–2008	108	**421**
9	Wasim Akram, Pakistan	1985–2002	104	**414**
10	Curtly Ambrose, West Indies	1988–2000	98	**405**

* As at 22 February 2008

The highest-placed Englishman is Ian Botham (11), with 383 wickets from 102 matches in the period 1977–92.

MOST RUNS IN A
TEST CRICKET CAREER*

	Player/country	Years	Matches	Innings	Runs
1	Brian Lara, West Indies†	1990–2006	131	232	**11,953**
2	Sachin Tendulkar, India	1989–2008	146	237	**11,150**
3	Allan Border, Australia	1978–94	156	265	**11,174**
4	Steve Waugh, Australia	1985–2004	168	260	**10,927**
5	Sunil Gavaskar, India	1971–87	125	214	**10,122**
6	Rahul Dravid, India†	1996–2008	119	205	**9,920**
7	Ricky Ponting, Australia	1995–2008	116	193	**9,776**
8	Jacques Kallis, South Africa	1995–2008	115	195	**9,431**
9	Graham Gooch, England	1975–95	118	215	**8,900**
10	Javed Miandad, Pakistan	1976–93	124	189	**8,832**

* As at 22 February 2008
† Includes runs made for ICC World XI in official Test Matches

Brian Lara made his Test debut in December 1990 against Pakistan in Lahore. He made 44 runs in the first innings and five in the second. His last Test was also against Pakistan, in Karachi in December 2006, when he scored 49 in his final innings.

MOST STANLEY CUP WINS*

	Team	First win	Last win	Total
1	Montreal Canadiens	1916	1993	24
2	Toronto Maple Leafs	1918	1967	13
3	Detroit Red Wings	1936	2002	10
4=	Boston Bruins	1929	1972	5
=	Edmonton Oilers	1984	1990	5
6=	New York Islanders	1980	1983	4
=	New York Rangers	1928	1994	4
=	Ottawa Senators	1920	1927	4
9=	Chicago Blackhawks	1934	1961	3
=	New Jersey Devils	1995	2003	3

* Since abolition of challenge match format in 1915; up to and including the 2007 Stanley Cup

During his time as Governor General of Canada from 1888 to 1893, Sir Frederick Arthur Stanley (Lord Stanley of Preston and 16th Earl of Derby) became interested in what is called hockey in the United States, and ice hockey elsewhere, and in 1893 presented a trophy to be contested by the best amateur teams in Canada. The first trophy went to the Montreal Amateur Athletic Association who won it without a challenge from any other team. In 1914 the Cup was contested by the champions of the National Hockey Association (formed 1910) and the Pacific Coast Hockey Association (formed 1912). Effectively it was a match between the champions of the East Coast and the West Coast. The NHA became the National Hockey League (NHL) in 1917 and their champions continued to play off against the PCHA champions. But in 1923 and 1924 it became a three-way challenge as a result of the formation of the Western Canadian Hockey League. The PCHA disbanded in 1926 and since then the NHL play-offs have decided the Stanley Cup finalists each spring.

MOST RUGBY LEAGUE CHALLENGE CUP FINAL WINS AT WEMBLEY*

	Club	First win	Last win	Total
1	Wigan	1929	1995	15
2	St Helens	1956	2007	8
3	Widnes	1930	1984	7
4	Leeds/Leeds Rhinos	1936	1999	6
5=	Castleford/Castleford Tigers	1935	1986	4
=	Wakefield Trinity	1946	1963	4
7=	Featherstone Rovers	1967	1983	3
=	Halifax	1931	1987	3
9=	Bradford Northern	1947	1949	2
=	Huddersfield	1933	1953	2
=	Warrington	1850	1974	2

* Up to and including 2007

The first final to be played at Wembley was on 4 May 1929, when Wigan beat Dewsbury 13–2 in front of 41,600 people. The first points at Wembley were scored by the legendary Wigan full back Jim Sullivan, when he kicked a goal after just four minutes. The first try was scored by Syd Abram, also of Wigan.

BIGGEST WINS IN THE SIX NATIONS CHAMPIONSHIP*

	Winner/loser	Year	Venue	Score
1	England vs. Italy	2001	Twickenham	80–23
2	Ireland vs. Italy	2000	Lansdowne Road	60–13
3	England vs. Italy	2000	Rome	59–12
4	France vs. Italy	2005	Rome	56–13
5	Ireland vs. Wales	2002	Lansdowne Road	54–10
6	France vs. Italy	2003	Rome	53–27
7	Ireland vs. Italy	2007	Rome	51–24
8	England vs. Italy	2004	Rome	50–9
9	England vs. Wales	2002	Twickenham	50–10
10	England vs. Ireland	2000	Twickenham	50–18

* Since 2000, when Italy joined the competition, based on the score of the winning team; up to and including the 2007 Championship

MOST POINTS IN A RUGBY UNION WORLD CUP CAREER

	Player	Country	Years	Points
1	Jonny Wilkinson	England	1999–2007	249
2	Gavin Hastings	Scotland	1987–95	227
3	Michael Lynagh	Australia	1987–95	195
4	Grant Fox	New Zealand	1987–91	170
5	Andrew Mehrtens	New Zealand	1995–9	163
6	Gonzalo Quesada	Argentina	1995–9	135
7	Matt Burke	Australia	1995–9	125
8	Thierry Lacroix	France	1991–5	124
9	Gareth Rees	Canada	1987–9	120
10	Chris Patterson	Scotland	2003–7	117

* Up to and including the 2007 tournament

Grant Fox scored 126 points in 1987, which represents the biggest haul in a single tournament.

MOST RACE WINS IN A FORMULA ONE CAREER BY A DRIVER*

	Driver/nationality	Years	Wins
1	Michael Schumacher, Germany	1992–2006	91
2	Alain Prost, France	1981–93	51
3	Ayrton Senna, Brazil	1985–93	41
4	Nigel Mansell, UK	1985–94	31
5	Jackie Stewart, UK	1965–73	27
6=	Jim Clark, UK	1962–8	25
=	Niki Lauda, Austria	1974–85	25
8	Juan-Manuel Fangio, Argentina	1950–57	24
9	Nelson Piquet, Brazil	1980–91	23
10	Damon Hill, UK	1993–8	22

* Up to and including the 2007 season

The most career wins by a current driver is 19 by Fernando Alonso (Spain).

THE 10
FIRST FORMULA ONE GRAND PRIX RACES OF LEWIS HAMILTON

	Grand Prix	Position	Date
1	Australian	3rd	18 Mar 2007
2	Malaysian	2nd	8 Apr 2007
3	Bahrain	2nd	15 Apr 2007
4	Spanish	2nd	3 May 2007
5	Monaco	2nd	7 May 2007
6	Canadian	1st	10 Jun 2007
7	United States	1st	17 Jun 2007
8	French	3rd	1 Jul 2007
9	British	3rd	8 Jul 2007
10	European	9th	22 Jul 2007

Hamilton started from fourth position on the grid in his debut race at Melbourne and went on to finish third behind eventual world champion Kimi Räikkönen (Finland) and his McLaren team-mate Fernando Alonso (Spain). Although Hamilton set an unprecedented record for a driver in his rookie season, his total of 12 podiums falls five short of the record set by Michael Schumacher in 2002.

DRIVERS WITH THE MOST FORMULA ONE WORLD TITLES*

	Driver/country	Years: first title/last title	Races won	World titles
1	Michael Schumacher, Germany,	1994–2004	91	7
2	Juan Manuel Fangio, Argentina	1951–7	24	5
3	Alain Prost, France	1985–93	51	4
4=	Jack Brabham, Australia	1959–60	14	3
=	Niki Lauda, Austria	1975–84	25	3
=	Nelson Piquet, Brazil	1981–7	23	3
=	Ayrton Senna, Brazil	1988–91	41	3
=	Jackie Stewart, UK	1969–71	27	3
9=	Alberto Ascari, Italy	1952–3	13	2
=	Jim Clark, UK	1963–5	25	2
=	Emerson Fittipaldi, Brazil	1972–4	14	2
=	Mika Hakkinen, Finland	1998–9	20	2
=	Graham Hill, UK	1962–8	14	2
=	Fernando Alonso, Spain	2005–6	19	2

* Up to and including the 2007 season

CONSTRUCTORS WITH THE MOST FORMULA ONE WORLD TITLES*

	Constructor/country	Years: first title/last title	Titles
1	Ferrari, Italy	1961–2007	15
2	Williams	1980–98	9
3	McLaren	1974–98	8
4	Lotus	1963–78	7
5=	Brabham	1966–7	2
=	Cooper	1959–60	2
=	Renault, France	2005–6	2
8=	Benetton	1995	1
=	BRM	1962	1
=	Matra, France	1969	1
=	Tyrrell	1971	1
=	Vanwall	1958	1

* Up to and including the 2007 season; all manufacturers UK unless otherwise stated

The world championship for drivers was launched in 1950, but not for constructors until 1958.

MOST WORLD MOTORCYCLING GRAND PRIX TITLES*

	Rider/country	Years	MotoGP 500cc	350cc	250cc	125cc	50/80cc	Total
1	Giacomo Agostini, Italy	1966 –75	8	7	0	0	0	**15**
2	Angel Nieto, Spain	1969 –84	0	0	0	7	6	**13**
3=	Carlo Ubbiali, Italy	1951 –60	0	0	3	6	0	**9**
=	Mike Hailwood, UK	1961 –67	4	2	3	0	0	**9**
5=	John Surtees, UK	1956 –60	4	3	0	0	0	**7**
=	Phil Read,UK	1964 –74	2	0	4	1	0	**7**
=	Valentino Rossi, Italy	1997– 2005	5	0	1	1	0	**7**

	Rider/country	Years	MotoGP 500cc	350cc	250cc	125cc	50/80cc	Total
8=	Geoff Duke, UK	1951 –55	4	2	0	0	0	**6**
=	Jim Redman, Southern Rhodesia	1962 –65	0	4	2	0	0	**6**
10=	Anton Mang, West Germany	1980 –87	0	2	3	0	0	**5**
=	Michael Doohan, Australia	1994 –98	5	0	0	0	0	**5**

* Solo classes only, up to and including the 2007 season

MOST MEN'S GRAND SLAM TITLES*

	Player/country	Years	Singles	Doubles	Mixed	Total
1	Roy Emerson, Australia	1959–71	12	16	0	**28**
2	John Newcombe, Australia	1965–76	7	17	2	**26**
3=	Frank Sedgman, Australia	1948–52	5	9	8	**22**
=	Todd Woodbridge, Australia	1988 –2004	0	16	6	**22**
5	Bill Tilden, USA	1913–30	10	6	5	**21**
6	Rod Laver, Australia	1960–71	11	6	3	**20**
7	John Bromwich, Australia	1938–50	2	13	4	**19**
8=	Jean Borotra, France	1925–36	4	9	5	**18**
=	Ken Rosewall, Australia	1953–72	8	9	1	**18**
=	Neale Fraser, Australia	1957–62	3	11	4	**18**

* Up to and including 2007

John Newcombe's total includes the 1965 Australian Open mixed doubles final, which was not played because of bad weather and the title was shared between the two pairs.

MOST WOMEN'S GRAND SLAM TITLES*

	Player/country	Years	Singles	Doubles	Mixed	Total
1	Margaret Court (née Smith), Australia)	1960–75	24	19	19	**62**
2	Martina Navratilova, Czechoslovakia/ USA	1974–2006	18	31	10	**59**
3	Bille Jean King (née Moffitt), USA	1961–81	12	16	11	**39**
4	Margaret Du Pont, USA	1941–62	6	21	10	**37**
5=	Louise Brough, USA	1942–57	6	21	8	**35**
=	Doris Hart, USA	1948–55	6	14	15	**35**
7	Helen Wills-Moody, USA	1923–38	19	9	3	**31**
8	Elizabeth Ryan, USA	1914–34	0	17	9	**26**
9=	Pam Shriver, USA	1981–7	0	22	1	**23**
=	Steffi Graf, Germany	1987–99	22	1	0	**23**

* Up to and including 2007

Suzanne Lenglen (France) won 21 Grand Slam events. If her 10 French titles, 1920–23, were included, she would appear on this list, but French Championships up to 1925 were for members of French clubs only, so are not considered official Grand Slam events.

MOST MEN'S SINGLES TITLES*

	Player/country	First win	Last win	Total wins
1	Jimmy Connors, USA	1972	1989	**109**
2	Ivan Lendl, Czechoslovakia/USA	1980	1993	**94**
3	John McEnroe, USA	1978	1991	**76**
4	Pete Sampras, USA	1990	2002	**64**
5	Guillermo Vilas, Argentina	1973	1983	**62**
6	Björn Borg, Sweden	1974	1981	**61**
7	Andre Agassi, USA	1987	2005	**60**
8	Ilie Nastase, Romania	1970	1978	**53**
9	Roger Federer, Switzerland	2001	2007	**52**
10	Boris Becker, Germany	1985	1996	**49**

* On the ATP Tour in the Open era 1968–2007
Source: ATP Tour

Connors's first title was in the 1972 Jacksonville Open, when he beat Clark Graebner (USA) 7–5, 6–4.

MOST WOMEN'S SINGLES TITLES*

	Player/country	First win	Last win	Total wins
1	Martina Navratilova, Czechoslovakia/USA	1974	1994	167
2	Chris Evert, USA	1971	1988	154
3=	Steffi Graf, Germany	1986	1999	107
=	Margaret Court (née Smith), Australia	1968	1976	107
5	Evonne Cawley (née Goolagong), Australia	1970	1980	68
6	Billie Jean King (née Moffitt), USA	1968	1983	67
7	Virginia Wade, UK	1968	1978	55
8=	Monica Seles, Yugoslavia/USA	1989	2002	53
=	Lindsay Davenport, USA	1993	2007	53
10	Martina Hingis, Switzerland	1995	2007	43

* On the WTA Tour in the Open era 1968–2007
Source: WTA Tour

FASTEST MEN OVER 100 METRES*

	Athlete/country	Venue	Date	Time (secs)
1	Asafa Powell, Jamaica	Rieti, Italy	9 Sep 2007	**9.74**
2	Justin Gatlin, USA	Doha, Qatar	12 May 2006	**9.77**
3	Maurice Greene, USA	Athens, Greece	16 Jun 1999	**9.79**
4=	Donovan Bailey, Canada	Atlanta, USA	27 Jul 1996	**9.84**
=	Bruny Surin, Canada	Seville, Spain	22 Aug 1999	**9.84**
=	Tyson Gay, USA	Zurich, Switzerland	18 Aug 2006	**9.84**
7=	Leroy Burrell, USA	Lausanne, Switzerland	6 Jul 2004	**9.85**
=	Olusoji A. Fasuba Nigeria	Doha, Qatar	12 May 2006	**9.85**
9=	Carl Lewis, USA	Tokyo, Japan	25 Aug 1991	**9.86**
=	Frank Fredericks, USA	Lausanne, Switzerland	3 Jul 1996	**9.86**
=	Ato Boldon, Trinidad	Walnut, USA	19 Apr 1998	**9.86**
=	Francis Obikwelu, Portugal	Athens, Greece	22 Aug 2004	**9.86**

* As at 1 January 2008
Source: IAAF

MOST MEN'S MAJORS IN A CAREER*

	Player/country	Years	US Masters	US Open	British Open	US PGA	Total
1	Jack Nicklaus	1962–86	6	4	3	5	**18**
2	Tiger Woods	1997–2007	4	2	3	4	**13**
3	Walter Hagen	1914–29	0	2	4	5	**11**
4=	Ben Hogan	1946–53	2	4	1	2	**9**
=	Gary Player, South Africa	1959–78	3	1	3	2	**9**
6	Tom Watson	1975–83	2	1	5	0	**8**
7=	Harry Vardon, England	1896–1914	0	1	6	0	**7**
=	Gene Sarazen	1922–35	1	2	1	3	**7**
=	Bobby Jones	1923–30	0	4	3	0	**7**
=	Sam Snead	1942–54	3	0	1	3	**7**
=	Arnold Palmer	1958–64	4	1	2	0	**7**

* Professional Majors only, up to and including 2007; all golfers from the USA unless otherwise stated

In 1930, Bobby Jones achieved an unprecedented Grand Slam when he won the US and British Open titles as well as the Amateur titles of both countries. Jack Nicklaus, Tiger Woods, Ben Hogan, Gary Player and Gene Sarazen are the only golfers to have won all four Majors at least once.

OLDEST GOLF CLUBS IN BRITAIN

	Club	Year formed
1	Royal Burgess Golfing Society of Edinburgh	1735
2	Honourable Company of Edinburgh Golfers (Muirfield)	1744
3	Royal and Ancient (St Andrews)	1754
4	Bruntsfield Links Golfing Society	1761
5	Royal Blackheath	1766
6	Royal Musselburgh	1774
7	Royal Aberdeen	1780
8=	Glasgow Gailes	1787
=	Glasgow Killermont	1787
10	Cruden Bay (Aberdeenshire)	1791

All these clubs are in Scotland with the exception of Royal Blackheath. The oldest in Northern Ireland is Royal Belfast (1881) and Ireland's oldest is Curragh, County Kildare (1883). The oldest Welsh club is Pontnewydd, Cwmbran (1875). The exact date of the formation of the Royal Blackheath Club is uncertain and some sources record that golf was played there in the 17th century by James I of England. However, it is generally accepted that the club was formed in 1766.

INDIVIDUAL SPORTS

CHAMPION JOCKEYS IN THE UK WITH THE MOST WINS IN A SEASON*

	Jockey	Season	Wins
1	Tony McCoy (NH)	2001–2	289
2	Gordon Richards (F)	1947	269
3	Gordon Richards (F)	1949	261
4	Gordon Richards (F)	1933	259
5	Tony McCoy (NH)	2002–3	256
6	Tony McCoy (NH)	1997–8	253
7	Fred Archer (F)	1885	246
8	Tony McCoy (NH)	1999–2000	245
9	Fred Archer (F)	1884	241
10	Frankie Dettori (F)	1994	233

* National Hunt (NH) and Flat racing (F) jockeys; totals as at end of 2007 flat racing season and the 2006–7 National Hunt season; all jockeys from the UK and Ireland except Frankie Dettori (Italy)

Seb Sanders and Jamie Spencer each rode 190 winners in 2007. It was the first time since 1923 that the flat racing title had been shared.

MOST WORLD PROFESSIONAL SNOOKER TITLES

	Player/country	Years	Wins
1	Ronnie O'Sullivan, England	2001, 2004, 2007	19
2	Joe Davis, England	1927–40, 1946	15
3=	John Pulman, England*	1964 (2), 1965 (3), 1966, 1968	7
=	Stephen Hendry, Scotland	1990, 1992–6, 1999	7
5=	Ray Reardon, Wales	1970, 1973–6, 1978	6
=	Steve Davis, England	1981, 1983, 1984, 1987–9	6
7=	Fred Davis, England†	1948–9, 1951	3
=	John Spencer, England	1969, 1971, 1977	3
9=	Walter Donaldson, Scotland	1947, 1950	2
=	Alex Higgins, Northern Ireland	1972, 1982	2
=	Mark Williams, Wales	2000, 2003	2
=	John Higgins, Scotland	1998, 2007	2

* Between 1964 and 1968 the championship was held on a challenge basis and John Pulman made two successful defences of the title in 1964, three in 1965 and one each in 1966 and 1968

† The World Championship was not held between 1953 and 1963; it was replaced by the Professional Match-Play Championship, which ran from 1952 to 1957. Fred Davis won the title five times, 1952–6, and John Pulman won it in 1957

ACKNOWLEDGEMENTS

Richard Braddish

Professor Cary Cooper, CBE

Russell E. Gough

Robert Grant

Harriet Harrison

Anthony Lipmann

Ian Morrison

Dafydd Rees

Robert Senior

Academy of Motion Picture Arts and Sciences

Adult Video News

artnet

Association of Leading Visitor Attractions

Association of Tennis Professionals

Audit Bureau of Circulations Ltd

BBC

The Bereavement Register

The Bookseller

Box Office Mojo

British Association of Aesthetic Plastic Surgeons

British Board of Film Censors

British Film Institute

British Video Association

BusinessWeek

CAMRA

Central Intelligence Agency

Checkout

Christie's

Cranfield University

Department for Environment, Food and Rural Affairs

Department of Health

The Economist

Emporis

Ethnologue

Euromonitor

Federal Bureau of Investigation

FHM

Financial Times

Food and Agriculture Organization of the United Nations

Football Writers' Association

Forbes

General Register Office for Scotland

Golden Raspberry Awards

Gold Fields Mineral Services

Hansard

HBOS

Home Accident Surveillance System

Home Office

Imperial War Museum

Interbrand

International Association of Athletics Federations

International Centre for Prison Studies

International Federation of Audit Bureaux of Circulations

International Game Fish Association

International Institute for Strategic Studies

International Monetary Fund

International Obesity Task Force

International Shark Attack File, Florida Museum of Natural History

International Telecommunication Union

Internet Movie Database

Internet World Stats

Interpol

iVillage

The Kennel Club

Kirin

Lipmann Walton

Live.com

Lycos 500™

Ministry of Justice

Miss World

MRIB

MSN UK

Music Information Database

National Basketball Association

National Football League

National Hockey League

National Phobics Society

National Statistics

AC Nielsen

Northern Ireland Statistics and Research Agency

The Official UK Charts Company

Organisation for Economic Co-operation and Development

Organisation Internationale des Constructeurs d'Automobiles

Oxford English Dictionary

PizzaExpress

Power & Motoryacht

Relate National Marriage Guidance

Royal Society for the Prevention of Cruelty to Animals

Savoy Hotel

Screen Digest

Society of Actuaries

Sotheby's

Sound Connection

Sunday Times

TNS Wordpanel

Transport for London

UMIST

United Nations

United Nations Population Division

US Census Bureau International Data Base

Ward's Motor Vehicle Facts & Figures 2007

Wine Institute

Wordtracker

World Bank

World Gold Council

World Health Organization

World Tennis Association

World Tourism Organization